PLATO'S
SHADOW

THE HELLENIZING
OF CHRISTIANITY

by Gary Petty

Little
Frog PUBLISHING

Printed in the United States of America

Scriptures quoted from The Holy Bible, New King James Version,
©1994 by Thomas Nelson, Inc.

Cover design by Rennie Palmer. Edited by Bill Palmer.

I offer special thanks to my wife Kim for her support in this endeavor and to Roger Foster
for his many hours of discussion on early church history. I also thank Dr. Ed Alcott and
Amanda Stiver for their input and suggestions.

CONTENTS

INTRODUCTION

Hebrew Scriptures predicted a Savior who would restore Israel to international prominence and establish the Kingdom of God over the entire world. Dignitaries from the East arrived in Judea telling of miraculous signs declaring the birth of this Jewish Messiah. The chance that the Messiah had arrived was too great a risk for King Herod to ignore. He issued orders to kill all Jewish male babies age two and under.

It was too late. Joseph, Mary and their infant son Jesus had already fled beyond the wailing sounds of distraught mothers. They joined a caravan meandering across the Sinai towards Egypt. Jesus would survive to return to Galilee and spend his youth working as a carpenter.

Around age 30, Jesus launched his career as an itinerant rabbi. His ministry lasted only three-and-a-half years before the Roman governor Pontius Pilate, under pressure from Jewish religious leaders, crucified him. In the face of opposition from both Romans and Jews, Jesus' followers spread his message across the Roman Empire. They claimed that Jesus was the prophesied Jewish Messiah and that he brought the way of eternal salvation to both Jew and non-Jew.

The earliest followers of Jesus of Nazareth are often called "Primitive Christians." Three centuries after Jesus a powerful church, claiming to be the successors of Jesus the Christ, became the dominant religion of the empire. By this time, early Christian doctrines and practices founded in the Hebrew Scriptures were mixed with Hellenistic culture and pagan customs. No longer was there a need to consider Jesus' teachings to "render unto Caesar the things which are Caesar's; and unto God the things which are God's" since the church and Roman Empire were inseparably linked.[1] Christianity in the 21st century is also experiencing dramatic changes. According to some pollsters, only a small minority of Christians in the United States today have the same biblical worldview as the majority of a few decades ago. In postmodern Europe, cathedrals stand as relics of a time when religion was a major influence in society.

Debates over multiculturalism, homosexuality, abortion, new methods of worship, and the legitimacy of distinct denominational doctrines are creating new Christian movements. While some believers flock to mega-churches with Broadway-style musical entertainment, others, jaded by stories about pedophile priests and a belief that the Bible is outmoded, talk of being "spiritual" rather than "religious."

Many Catholics in Europe and the United States question orthodox positions on such important issues as abortion and homosexuality. Mainline Protestant churches are losing members to more charismatic, evangelical movements. Groups such as the Mormons and Jehovah's Witnesses, once considered fringe cults, now number their followers in the millions.

What does post-modern Christianity have in common with the teachings of Jesus, who walked the dusty roads of Judea and Galilee 2,000 years ago? To understand where Christianity is headed, we must first look at the development of the Christian religion in the three centuries following its founding by Jesus of Nazareth.

This book is an attempt to discover elements of what is commonly called Primitive Christianity. In it we will explore a brief overview of the Jewish and Roman world of the early Christians and what the earliest followers of Jesus believed about the afterlife, the Ten Commandments, the Passover, baptism and idolatry. We will explore Christianity's Jewish roots and the manner in which early Christian groups became influenced by Greek philosophy. The story is complicated, and sometimes bizarre, but important to examine if we are to understand the future of Christianity. It is important for anyone who desires to be a true disciple of Jesus Christ.

1

A JEWISH SECT
IN AN OUTPOST
OF THE EMPIRE

Early Christianity experienced remarkable growth as the disciples of Jesus of Nazareth spread his teachings throughout the Roman Empire. Jesus' followers soon discovered that success created its own difficulties. Within a few years after their Messiah's death, Christians suffered intense persecution from Jews, pagans and the Roman government. Internal struggles fragmented the Church into competing sects. The scattered congregations underwent such dramatic changes that toward the end of the first century, a church leader named Diotrephes rejected Jesus' beloved apostle John as a Christian teacher.[1]

The diversity of Christian teachings that developed over the next century was staggering. During its first decades, Christianity existed as a Jewish sect. The primary message was the declaration of Jesus as the Messiah, the call for personal repentance, and the good news of Jesus' return to establish the Kingdom of God on earth. The earliest Christians hotly debated circumcision and other

Jewish customs, questioning whether they were required for non-Jews, or Gentiles. Over time more controversies rose. Converts debated whether Jesus had a real body, or was an apparition? Schisms formed over the question of whether Christians should observe Passover or Easter. Various groups, today labeled by scholars as gnostics, argued that there were multiple gods including the God of the Old Testament and a separate supreme god revealed by Jesus. Asceticism inspired some believers to reject all human pleasures and comforts. Other individuals claimed that

---

Important Historical Sources

Philo: A first century Jewish writer from Alexandria, Egypt who combined Greek philosophy with his interpretation of the Hebrew Scriptures. Philo was impressed with the teachings of the Pythagoreans and Plato. He taught an allegorical interpretation of the Bible along with the Hellenistic concept of the immortality of the soul.

Josephus: Flavius Josephus (c. 37-95 AD) was a Jewish military commander and historian. He commanded Jewish troops during the revolt against the Romans (66-70 AD). After being captured by the Romans, Josephus became convinced that the Jews could not defeat Rome and became an interpreter for his former enemies. Later, he wrote *The Jewish Wars* and *The Jewish Antiquities*.

Tacitus: This Roman historian (c. 55-117 AD) recorded details of Roman life in *The Annals of Imperial Rome* and other works. He mentions both Christ as the founder of the Christians and Pontius Pilate as the Roman governor who killed him. [2]

Suetonius: Suetonius (c. 69-140 AD), was an imperial secretary under Emperor Hadrian with access to many official documents. These documents supplied the groundwork for his book, *The Lives of the Twelve Caesars*.

---

the discovery of true spirituality lay in total abandonment to the senses. To understand how Christianity changed and fragmented, we must first understand the world in which it grew.

The Roman World

Between the birth of Jesus, and the death of the last of his original apostles, the Roman Empire extended from the Euphrates River to the Atlantic Ocean and from the North Sea to the Sahara Desert in North Africa. Various estimates put the population between 50 and 80 million people.

The Romans bridged cultures by constructing thousands of miles of roads, developing a postal system and expanding trade. Commerce flourished between far-flung points on the Roman map, and wealth poured into the capital city of Rome. Roman law created order and afforded some safety for travelers. The status of a Roman citizen afforded numerous legal rights. Paul of Tarsus, the first century's greatest Christian missionary, used his Roman citizenship on numerous occasions to save himself from violent persecution.[3]

The empire's policies were generally tolerant of local customs and religions as long as they did not interfere with Roman laws and political aims. Subjugated people were allowed to continue their religious practices, although forming new religions was discouraged. Judaism was accepted as a legitimate religion with ancient temple rituals and Scriptures.

The Greek pantheon, with Roman names attached to Greek gods and goddesses, formed the traditional Roman religion. Religious openness allowed the propagation of diverse beliefs and practices, including Persian Mithraism and Babylonian mystery cults. A temple to the Egyptian goddess Isis was found in the ruins of the Roman city Pompeii, which was destroyed by the eruption of Mount Vesuvius in 79 AD. The pagan world of the first century was a mixture of institutionalized cults, local gods and goddesses, temple prostitution, astrology and superstitious belief in magic.

All of these beliefs flourished under the overriding umbrella of emperor worship.

This religious pluralism created a dynamic environment in which the common person was receptive to new religious ideas. This fertile ground accelerated the spread of Christianity.

The Romans also adopted a great deal of Greek culture as their own. Greek was the common language of commerce and education. Roman conquerors overlaid a veneer of Hellenistic culture on every nation absorbed into the empire.

The Jewish World

Judaism of the first century was a product of over 2,000 years of history. The Jews proudly traced their origins to the biblical patriarchs and events of the Egyptian Exodus, after which God instituted a covenant with their forefathers. Around 1446 BC, Moses led Israel out of Egypt, and after 40 years of wandering in the wilderness, to the land of Canaan on the eastern edge of the Mediterranean. For hundreds of years the 12 tribes formed a loose confederation before becoming a unified kingdom ruled by King Saul around 1050 BC. Under Kings David and Solomon, almost a millennium before the Roman occupation, Israel was an important power in the Middle East.

After Solomon's reign, the nation split into two kingdoms. The Assyrians eventually conquered the Northern Kingdom. For decades after the fall of the Northern Kingdom, the southern Jewish kingdom played a dangerous game of international political gamesmanship, leading to Babylonian invasion.

When Jerusalem fell to the Babylonians in 586 BC, the Jewish people were deported to destinations throughout the Babylonian-Chaldean Empire. In c. 539 BC, Cyrus, king of Persia, conquered Babylon. The Persians allowed many peoples scattered by the Babylonians, including the Jews, to return to their homelands.[4]

Before the captivity, the center of Jewish religious life was Solomon's grand temple in Jerusalem. When the Jews returned to their homeland under the leadership of Zerubbabel, they constructed a new temple, although it was a shadow of its former glory.

Not all Jews chose, nor had the opportunity, to leave the places where they had settled. Many remained scattered throughout the Persian Empire, left behind as the people of the *Diaspora*, or dispersion. Since it was impossible for far-flung Jewish communities to participate in Jerusalem temple worship, here the synagogue became the center of Jewish communal life. The synagogue was a place for prayer, for study of the Hebrew Scriptures, for social activities and for religious services. The presence of synagogues in cities throughout the Roman Empire produced a receptive audience to the message of the first Christian missionaries. On many occasions, the apostle Paul introduced the Christian message in a new city by first teaching in a Jewish synagogue.[5]

Although the Persians had allowed the Jews to return home as vassals of their empire, the children of Abraham eventually found themselves under the not-so-easygoing control of the Macedonian-Greek Empire, and later the Ptolemies and Seleucids. The Jews regained autonomy through a war of independence between 167 and 141 BC. Judea was then governed by a succession of rulers known as the Hasmoneans until the Romans, under Pompey, took control in 63 BC. Julius Caesar placed an Idumean named Antipater as king of Judea.[6] In 37 BC, Antipater's son, known as Herod the Great, succeeded his father as ruler.

Herod was an ambitious builder who remodeled Zerubbabel's temple, built the remarkable harbor at Caesarea, and constructed magnificent fortresses, including Masada. Herod was also a vicious tyrant who murdered members of his own family and executed anyone whom he perceived as a threat. When Herod the Great died in 4 BC, his kingdom was divided among family members. Eventually, the area known as Judea was ruled by a Roman governor stationed in Caesarea.[7]

At the time of Jesus, Jewish political and religious life centered around Herod's temple. The Romans allowed the Jews to govern their own internal affairs, under the watchful eye of the Roman governor. The Sanhedrin, comprised of 70 members, including priests, other religious leaders and aristocrats, was the ruling political and religious council.

Romans and Jews

Flavius Josephus (c. 37-95 AD) records that both Julius Caesar and Augustus Caesar gave special privileges to the Jews throughout the empire. In *Antiquities of the Jews* Josephus tells of the Jewish leader Hycranus, who aligned himself with Julius Caesar. During a battle, Hycranus arrived at a crucial moment with 1,500 Jewish soldiers to assure a Roman victory. As a reward, Caesar declared that Hycranus and his descendants would serve as the high priests in the Jerusalem temple. Official decrees protected the Jewish observance of the sabbatical year and permitted Jewish holy days to be celebrated in Rome itself.[8]

Julius Caesar's successor, Augustus, responded to Greek persecution of the Jews by issuing more decrees on their behalf, including one offering protection against having to appear before civil judges on the Sabbath. In addition, Roman law protected Jewish "holy books" and "sacred money" in synagogues and schools.[9] These imperial favors did not always reflect the perceptions of other Romans.

Jewish origins were debated by Roman historians. Some believed that the Israelites originated in Crete, Ethiopia or an ancient country mentioned by the Greek poet Homer. One theory claimed that at one time the Jews were lepers who originated in Egypt. In this scenario, an Egyptian pharaoh was inspired by an oracle to drive them into a foreign land because they were under a divine curse. Eating pigs had caused the leprosy, so the Jews avoided consuming swine's flesh.

The Roman historian Tacitus (c. 55-117 AD) wrote that the origins of the Jews could be traced to a time when they lived in Egypt, but that the Egyptians expelled them because they suffered from a dreaded disease. They would have died in the wilderness were it not for the leadership of a man named Moses, who then gave them a unique religion.

Jewish religious observances seemed bizarre to most Romans. Some Romans maintained that Jewish customs originated in older religions. Misconceptions included the belief that the sacrifice of bulls in the Jerusalem temple originated in the cult of the Egyptian god Apis and the observance of the seventh-day Sabbath came from an ancient belief in the god Saturn. The most unique Jewish doctrine, and one that baffled the Romans, was the insistence on one God so transcendent that he forbade the use of idols. Tacitus described Jewish religion as "sinister" and "revolting." He condemned the Jewish refusal to intermarry, or even to eat meals with other peoples.[10] Seneca (c. 6 BC-65 AD), a Roman Stoic philosopher, chided Jews for Sabbath observance because the practice caused them to waste one seventh of their lives.[11]

The relationship between Romans and Jews was at times cordial, but at other times tumultuous. Augustus' successor Tiberius forbade all Jewish religious practices in Rome, ordering Jewish sacred vestments and utensils burned.[12] Emperor Claudius eventually ordered all Jews out of the city in 49 AD.[13]

Complexity of First Century Judaism

In the *Diaspora*, the *Torah* became the glue binding Jewish people and culture. The Hebrew word "torah" means "instruction" or "teaching" and is often translated "law." Jewish tradition taught that the written *Torah*, referring to the first five books of the Hebrew Scriptures—Genesis, Exodus, Leviticus, Numbers and Deuteronomy—was penned mostly by Moses. The *Torah* contains both stories that reveal God's interaction with humanity and his laws that He gave to Israel.[14] Jewish religious leaders also amassed oral traditions that were passed down from generation to generation.

Jewish Groups of the First Century

Pharisees: Believed in a strict interpretation of the *Torah*, followed the oral law, looked for the Messiah and taught the resurrection from the dead. A number of Pharisees joined the Christian sect after accepting Jesus as the Messiah. Among these Pharisees was the famous Apostle Paul.

Sadducees: A group made up of temple priests and members of the wealthy class. The Sadducees adhered to the books of Moses, but did not ascribe authority to the rest of the Hebrew Scriptures. They were in conflict with the Pharisees over interpretation of the *Torah* and understanding of doctrines such as the resurrection of the dead.

Herodians: A political party that supported the Herod family.

Zealots: A group exhibiting an intense religious desire for independence from Roman rule.

Essenes: Though not mentioned in the Bible, this group was important in Jewish society of the first century. They were concerned with moral and ritual purity in preparation for the future Messianic rule. Most historians credit the Essenes with writing the *Dead Sea Scrolls*.

At the end of the Babylonian Exile, as large numbers of Jews returned to their homeland, there was intense interest in protecting the national religion by developing a system of worship and study of the *Torah*. Scripture had to be copied and order created from the mass of oral *halakhah*—ritual and moral laws designed to govern every aspect of Jewish life. These laws had accumulated over the centuries. Scribes, trained in both the oral and written law, became important figures in Judaism.[15] The biblical Ezra is considered the greatest of these scribes.[16]

Religious leaders sought to discover how the *Torah* was to guide every detail of daily life. New oral laws were established, principles expounded, and meanings of words explored. In this manner, the oral traditions became an ever-expanding legal code.

The Jewish religious teachers of the third century before the birth of Jesus were known as the "fathers." One of their traditions stated, "Be deliberate in passing judgment, and raise up many disciples, and build a hedge around the Law."[17]

This hedge was to be a defense of the *Torah* of God through a system of oral *halakhah* that protected the written laws. It is this system of oral law, with its interpretation of the *Torah*, that the Apostle Paul calls "the tradition of my fathers."[18] The oral law was esteemed by many, including the Pharisees, with the same reverence as the written law. It could be claimed that it was the unwritten code that insured Israel's distinction among the nations.

Philo, a first century Jewish writer from Alexandria, Egypt described the importance of the oral law among Jews living outside of Judea: "For the man who obeys the written laws is not justly entitled to any praise, inasmuch as he is influenced by compulsion and the fear of punishment. But he who abides by the unwritten laws is worthy of praise, as exhibiting a spontaneous and unconstrained virtue."[19] During the early life of Jesus, the prominent study of the *Torah* and oral law was centered in two schools founded by Hillel and Shammai.

Our understanding of the diversity in first century Judaism is enhanced by the discovery of the *Dead Sea Scrolls* in 1947. Scores of scrolls in both Hebrew and Aramaic, dating from 250 BC to 70 AD, were uncovered in caves around Qumran. These writings are often attributed to the most exclusive of the Jewish religious groups known as the Essenes.

The First Christians

It was in Roman-occupied Judea that the followers of Jesus of Nazareth, consisting mainly of Jews, claimed to have a unique relationship with the God of Israel. They announced that Jesus was the prophesied Messiah and invited all peoples to join them in this special relationship. Their radical message declared that the God of Israel was inviting all mankind to know him as their Creator.

Soon, this small Jewish sect spread their message beyond the borders of Judea to the synagogues of the *Diaspora*. They collected letters and books written by Jesus' followers into a new set of Scriptures. The Jesus sect didn't fade like so many other Messianic groups. Non-Jews began to respond and small Christian congregations sprang up all over the Roman Empire.

To understand early Christianity we must first understand the Jewish culture in which it was born, the Greek world it confronted and the Roman Empire where it grew.

2

THE GOD OF ABRAHAM, ISAAC AND JACOB

Ask a Jew of the first century about his history and religion and the answer would have been direct and simple. The Jews were the descendants of Abraham, Isaac and Jacob, the people chosen by God to receive the *Torah* through Moses. First century Jews insisted that no other gods existed except the one God of Israel. This monotheistic identity was burned into their minds and hearts.

The Hebrew Scriptures tell the story of how the God of Abraham was the Creator of all physical matter and spirit beings called angels. He created the first two humans in his "image" and "likeness," then placed them in a garden named Eden. An angel, who had rejected God, deceived Adam and Eve into disobeying their Creator. Consequently, the first humans were driven from Eden.

God told these first humans that they were made of the dust, and that because of their rebellion, they would die and return to dust. For many centuries humans stubbornly lived without regard for God. The biblical book of Genesis relates just two major interventions by God in the first centuries of human existence. First, God set in motion the great Deluge as a punishment on an evil humanity. Centuries later, God confused the human languages at the tower of Babel to prevent Nimrod from creating a world empire.[1]

The Jews traced their history to a time more than 2,000 years before Jesus, when a caravan meandered into Canaan on the eastern shores of the Mediterranean. A man named Abram and his wife Sarai received a miraculous message from God, who told them to leave their home in Ur in the land of the Chaldeans between the Tigris and Euphrates Rivers. Once Abram arrived in Canaan, he received God's promise that he and Sarai would become the parents of a great people. God then changed their names to Abraham and Sarah. He also promised Abraham that all nations would be blessed through him.[2]

It was when God initiated a covenant with Abraham that he began to reveal his plan to save rebellious humanity. This covenant was confirmed with Abraham's son Isaac, Isaac's son Jacob (later named Israel), and Jacob's 12 sons. Abraham's descendants became known as Hebrews or Israelites. During the life of Jacob a famine forced the Israelites to migrate into Egypt, where over the course of centuries their numbers grew and they were enslaved by the Egyptians.[3]

God eventually called a man named Moses to lead the Israelites back to the land of Canaan. When pharaoh refused to free the Israelites, God poured out 10 disastrous plagues on the Egyptians. Pharaoh was forced to free the slaves, who by this time numbered in the millions.[4] God then led the Israelites from Egypt with a pillar of fire by night and a pillar of smoke by day. When Israel came to the impassable Red Sea, God parted the waters to allow them through, and then closed it on the pursuing Egyptian army.

The Israelites trekked to Mount Sinai, where God appeared in a fiery cloud and declared them to be a nation of "kings and priests." Moses was summoned to the summit of Mount Sinai to receive Ten Commandments on two tablets of stone. These commandments formed the basis of God's covenant with Israel as the descendants of Abraham.[5]

The Israelites repeatedly rebelled against Moses' leadership and God denied the generation who left Egypt the opportunity to enter the land promised to Abraham. After 40 years of wandering in the desert, a younger generation entered Canaan. During those years of Israel's wandering, God instructed them to create a priesthood and gave them an elaborate set of laws dealing with everything from morality, health, sex, property rights and holy days. The laws also provided regulations for Israel to function as a nation.

Teachings from the *Torah*

A summary of the Ten Commandments:

1. Worship only the One God.

2. Do not use images in the worship of God.

3. Do not use God's name in vain.

4. Remember and honor the Sabbath day.

5. Honor your father and mother.

6. Do not murder.

7. Do not commit adultery.

8. Do not steal.

9. Do not lie.

10. Do not covet what others have. [6]

"Hear, O Israel: The LORD our God, the LORD is one! You shall love the LORD your God with all your heart, with all your soul, and with all your strength." [7]

"You shall not take vengeance, nor bear any grudge against the children of your people, but you shall love your neighbor as yourself: I am the LORD." [8]

"At the end of every seven years you shall grant a release of debts." [9]

"There shall not be found among you anyone who makes his son or his daughter pass through the fire, or one who practices witchcraft, or a soothsayer, or one who interprets omens, or a sorcerer, or one who conjures spells, or a medium, or a spiritist, or one who calls up the dead." [10]

"One witness shall not rise up against a man concerning any iniquity or any sin that he commits; by the mouth of two or three witnesses the matter shall be established." [11]

"You shall not see your brother's donkey or his ox fall along the road, and hide yourself from them; you shall surely help him lift them up again." [12]

"You shall not charge interest to your brother—interest on money or food or anything that is lent out at interest. To a foreigner you may charge interest, but to your brother you shall not charge interest..." [13]

"When you reap your harvest in your field, and forget a sheaf in the field, you shall not go back to get it; it shall be for the stranger, the fatherless, and the widow, that the LORD your God may bless you in all the work of your hands. When you beat your olive trees, you shall not go over the boughs again; it shall be for the stranger, the fatherless, and the widow." [14]

"You shall not lie with a male as with a woman. It is an abomination." [15]

The Israelite View of God and Government

Yahweh, the God of Israel, was a personal being. At Sinai the people saw his power in a fiery cloud and heard the thunder of a voice giving the Ten Commandments.

While Moses was on Mount Sinai receiving the commandments, many Israelites rebelled against *Yahweh* by worshipping the image of a golden calf. One tribe, the Levites, had not participated in the rebellion and God selected them as his priests. (Originally, God had not created a unique priesthood, but instructed each head of a household to offer an animal sacrifice as an act of worship.)[16] Moses was instructed to construct a tabernacle with an elaborate sacrificial system.[17] Once the tabernacle was completed, the cloud of the "glory of the LORD" filled it as a visual reminder that Israel was the people of God's special presence, a phenomenon the rabbis called *shekinah*.[18] Around four-and-a-half centuries after Moses built the tabernacle, Solomon erected a temple to *Yahweh* in Jerusalem. At the dedication ceremony this cloud of the "glory of the LORD" filled Solomon's temple.[19]

Not only was *Yahweh* a personal God who interacted with his people, but he chose individuals to receive his *ruach*, or Spirit. When God's Spirit came upon these chosen ones, they became his special messengers and prophets.[20]

God intended Israel's government to be a theocracy, although it rarely functioned as one. The system originally consisted of a political leader (Moses) and a high priest (Moses' brother Aaron). The day-to-day administration of government was carried out locally through tribal elders and priests. After they entered Canaan, the Israelites were a loose confederation of tribes ruled by "judges" until they united under the monarchies of kings Saul, David and Solomon.

An important aspect of Israelite government was the concept of the rule of law. The *Torah* commanded the king not to use his position to gain great wealth. He was also instructed to write down

Israel's History

c. 2100-1800 BC Abraham and Sarah enter Canaan. Abraham's son Isaac declared the son of promise. Isaac's son Jacob has 12 sons. Jacob's son Joseph is sold into slavery but ends up as a governor in Egypt.

c. 1446 BC Moses leads the Israelites out of Egypt and back into the Promised Land.

c. 1406 BC After wandering in the wilderness for 40 years, the Israelites entered Canaan under the leadership of Joshua.

c. 1406-1050 BC Joshua conquers most of Canaan. Israel is a loose confederation of 13 tribes ruled by judges.

c. 1050 BC Saul becomes the first king of Israel.

c. 1010 BC David becomes king of Judah, then king of a united Israel seven-and-a-half years later.

c. 970 BC David's son Solomon becomes king of Israel.

c. 959 BC Solomon completes the temple in Jerusalem.

c. 930 BC The nation divides into the northern kingdom of Israel with its capital in Samaria and the southern kingdom of Judah with its capital in Jerusalem.

722 BC The northern kingdom of Israel is destroyed by the Assyrians.

586 BC The southern kingdom of Judah is destroyed by the Babylonians.

538 BC Jewish captives begin to return to Judah.

516 BC Zerubbabel constructs a second temple.

169 BC Antiochus Epiphanies IV sacks Jerusalem. In 166 BC the Jews revolted under the leadership of Judas Maccabeus, gaining independence 25 years later.

37 BC Herod the Great becomes king of Judea. In 20 BC he began to remodel the temple in Jerusalem. Herod's temple was one of the great wonders of its day. (The Judea of Herod the Great included territories that the Romans separated from the province of Judea when Herod died. Galilee and Perea went to Herod Antipas; Herod Archelaus took Judea, Samaria and Edema; Philip ruled the territories north and east of Galilee, and directly north of the Decapolis. Christ was born in Judea, and at the time of His birth, Nazareth was part of Judea. When Joseph and Mary brought Christ back to Nazareth, the city was no longer part of Judea, but part of Galilee.

c. 4 BC Birth of Jesus.

---

a copy of the *Torah* and to study it all his life "that he may learn to fear the LORD his God and be careful to observe all the words of this law and these statues, that his heart may not be lifted above his brethren, that he may not turn aside from the commandment to the right hand or to the left...."[21] This concept of the rule of divine law was markedly different from the tyranny that existed in much of the ancient world.

Essential in the worship of *Yahweh* was avoiding other religions. Israel was forbidden to adopt the idolatry and worship customs of other tribes and nations. The law specifically condemned the practice of witchcraft and use of spiritual mediums. In this way the people of Israel were to be the unique representatives of God to all nations.[22]

The Messianic Kingdom

In Deuteronomy, Moses declared blessings the Israelites would receive for obeying their covenant with God and curses that would befall them if they failed. Then, in a series of statements that must have been shocking to his audience, Moses prophesied that in the future Israel would break the covenant and be destroyed as a nation. The children of Abraham would be scattered among many nations until they turned back to God, at which point he would gather them back into the Promised Land.[23]

The biblical story of Israel is the recurring cycle of the nation sliding into disobedience to God's covenant, followed by a call from judges, priests and prophets to repent. The refusal to repent brought divine punishment; divine punishment created oppression and poverty; the suffering from this punishment motivated national repentance; and then God restored the nation to his favor. God sent to his people "anointed ones," who served as rulers or prophets, to lead Israel back into a relationship with him. The Hebrew Scriptures also contain prophecies of a specific "Anointed One," or Messiah, who would someday serve God as the supreme King of Israel.

The prophet Isaiah, whose career covered a tumultuous period in Israel's history between c. 740 and 680 BC, proclaimed detailed prophecies about the future Messianic Kingdom. According to Isaiah, the Messiah will rule the nations from Jerusalem, where all people will come to worship the true God. The *Torah* of God will be taught to the Gentiles, the Messiah will settle disputes between nations, and instruments of war will be reconstructed into farming tools.[24]

The Messiah is to be a descendant of King David and have the Spirit of God, which will impart to him "wisdom and understanding...counsel and might...knowledge and fear of the LORD." The children of Abraham will be gathered to the Promised Land again, then the Messiah will rule with fairness as all nations seek to follow him. Even the nature of animals will be changed. The lion will lie down with the lamb, and the cow and the bear will graze together.[25]

One prophecy proclaimed, "For unto us a Child is born, unto us a Son is given; and the government will be upon His shoulder. And His name will be called Wonderful, Counselor, Mighty God, Everlasting Father, Prince of Peace. Of the increase of His government and peace there will be no end. Upon the throne of David and over His Kingdom, to order it and establish it with judgment and justice, from that time forward, even forever."[26]

Isaiah also told of a Suffering Servant. This Anointed One of God would look like a common person, but be tortured and die for the sins of the people. God would accept this Servant's death as a sacrifice for the sins of others.[27]

The Resurrection of the Dead

A unique teaching of the Old Testament was that death was an unconscious state in which a person waited for a resurrection back to life at the coming of the Messiah. From the Babylonian captivity the prophet Daniel wrote, "And many who sleep in the dust of the earth shall awake, some to everlasting life, some to shame and everlasting contempt."[28]

The Hebrew Scriptures taught that both human beings and animals are *nephesh* (translated "soul" in English Bibles), which means "a breathing creature." The English word "soul" is often tainted with the Greek idea of immortality. This concept is absent in *nephesh*, which denotes life, but has no connection to immortality.[29] In the Hebrew Scriptures the dead, both the good and the evil, go to *sheol. Sheol* is synonymous with an earthen grave.[30] Israel's King David lamented that in *sheol* there is no remembrance of God.[31]

David's son, King Solomon, summed up the helplessness of death in sheol in Ecclesiastes 9:5-6: "For the living know that they will die; but the dead know nothing, and they have no more reward, for the memory of them is forgotten. Also their love, their hatred, and their envy have now perished; nevermore will they have a share in anything done under the sun."

He continues his gloomy commentary in verse 10: "Whatever your hand finds to do, do it with all your might; for there is no work or device or knowledge or wisdom in the grave where you are going."

The Old Testament contains repeated promises of a future resurrection to life. In the book of Job, the suffering righteous man lamented that he would be hidden in *sheol* until God called him back to life. Similarly, the psalmist declared "God will redeem my soul from the power of the grave."[32]

This resurrection was linked to the Messianic Kingdom. Isaiah wrote of a future day of salvation for the people of Judah: "Your dead shall live; together with my dead body they shall arise. Awake and sing, you who dwell in the dust; for your dew is like the dew of herbs, and the earth will cast out the dead."[33]

The prophet Ezekiel (c. 571 BC) recorded a vision in which he found himself in a large valley filled with dry bones representing all the Israelites who had ever lived. In the vision the bones are given flesh and are brought back to life. God then declared to the prophet, "O my people, I am going to open your graves and bring you up from them; I will bring you back to the land of Israel."[34] Ezekiel also prophesied a time when Israel and Judah would be reunited and David would once again reign as their king.[35]

The prophets proclaimed that the Messiah was coming to bring all people to God, and Israel would play a special part in that kingdom as the children of Abraham, the chosen ones, unique in all human history.

In the first century AD, the descendants of Abraham, laboring under the heel of the Roman Empire, anxiously anticipated the Messiah's arrival to rule the world from Jerusalem. Some Jews applied the prophecies concerning the Messiah, Isaiah's prophesied Child who is the Prince of Peace, the Son of David and the Suffering Servant, to a carpenter-from-Galilee-turned-itinerant-preacher named Jesus.

The Israelite Concept of the Soul

In Genesis 2:7 God "breathes" into the first man and he becomes nephesh. Nephesh is also translated "creature" in reference to animals in Genesis 1:24, and "body" in Leviticus 21:11 in reference to a dead carcass.

The Jewish Encyclopedia.com states: "The belief that the soul continues its existence after death is a matter of philosophical and theological speculation rather than of simple truth, and it is accordingly nowhere expressly taught in the Holy Scripture. As long as the soul was conceived to be merely a breath, and not inseparably connected, if not identified, with the life blood, no real substance could be ascribed to it. As soon as the spirit or breath of God, which was believed to keep body and soul together, both in man and in beast, is taken away, the soul goes down to Sheol or Hades, there to live a shadowy existence without life and consciousness."[36]

Jerusalem

Jerusalem, for three of the world's largest religions, is one of the holiest places on earth. For Jews it is where Solomon's Temple was a place of God's special presence. Jerusalem is where Muslims believe Mohammed ascended into heaven to receive instructions from Allah. Christians believe that Jesus Christ, the Son of God, was crucified and resurrected in this ancient city. Egyptians, Assyrians, Babylonians, Greeks, Romans, Arabs, Christian crusaders and Turks have shed blood to possess Jerusalem.

References to the city of Jerusalem are found in Egyptian writings dating back to the 1700s and 1800s BC. Some historians trace the origins of the city's name to a local god named Shalem. Salem in Hebrew means "peace," and over time Jerusalem became interpreted as "city of peace."[37]

When Israel invaded Canaan under the leadership of Joshua, Jerusalem was a city-state occupied by the Jebusites, whom he never totally drove out of the area.[38]

The southern part of city of the Jebusites was situated on a steep hill called Zion. Here the they built a fortress, which was conquered by King David.[39] David brought the ark of the covenant into this part of Jerusalem and it became known as the City of David. Over time, the City of David and Zion became interchangeable terms.

Solomon built the temple to *Yahweh* on Mount Moriah, which lies just to the north of Mount Zion.[40] Mount Moriah was important in Israelite history as the place where Abraham took his son Isaac to sacrifice him according to God's instructions. Mount Moriah is also where God ordered David to erect an altar in his honor.[41]

Eventually, the area encompassing the City of David, the Temple Mount and the city of Jerusalem become known as Zion. In Psalm 2 King David prophesied that the Messiah would reign from Zion.

3

PYTHAGORAS, PLATO, PHILO AND PHILOSOPHY

In the first half of the fifth century BC, the Jews were struggling to rebuild their homeland. Many still resided in the lands of their former Babylonian masters, though Persians now ruled those territories.

At the same time, on a peninsula jutting into the northern Mediterranean, a group of city states united to face the mighty Persian Empire. The Hellenes, or Greeks, under the leadership of city states Athens and Sparta, fought and eventually defeated the huge Persian army in battles that are still glorified in Western Civilization—Marathon, Thermopylae, and Salamis.

Before the Persian wars, Athens experienced its golden age. Trends that had been growing in Greek culture culminated in an Athenian epoch of creative innovations in architecture, medicine, epic writing, poetry, sculpture, dramatic and comedic plays, astronomy and government. The innovations in government laid the foundations of democracy.

Every male citizen was a member of the *Ecclesia* (Assembly), which met about 40 times a year to make political decisions. There was another body of 500 men, called the *Boule*, who dealt with the day-to-day business of the government.[1] Slaves had no rights, and citizenship was withheld from women, but every free Athenian male enjoyed voting privileges.

While Sparta developed a military culture, Athens became a trading and seafaring power with a strong navy. Greek city states spread Hellenistic culture by colonizing towns on the shores of the Aegean and Mediterranean Seas.

The Greeks believed in the development of both mind and body. They founded academies for teaching language, mathematics and the arts. Athletes from all over Greece competed in sporting games honoring the gods. The greatest of these events was the Olympics, held every four years.

Greek religion was based in the belief that the gods and goddesses lived on Mount Olympus. The chief Grecian god was Zeus, who ruled over an array of super beings who displayed all-too-human frailties. Athena was the goddess of wisdom and household crafts. Apollo, the sun god, was the patron of music, archery, medicine and truth. Poseidon was the god of the seas. Artemis was a virgin goddess who protected cities, animals and women. Aphrodite was the goddess of love and beauty, and Hermes was the messenger of Zeus. The gods and goddesses were said to give cryptic messages to mortals through oracles. The most famous of these oracles spoke from the temple at Delphi.

The Peloponnesian War, a conflict between Greek city states from 431-404 BC, threatened to destroy the Athenian renaissance. However, the Greek cultural spirit was forever embedded in the future of the Mediterranean.

The Golden Age of Greek Philosophy

Around 530 BC a philosophy based on the teachings of a philosopher named Pythagoras was thriving in a Corinthian

---

Important Greeks

Homer (eighth century BC): Name given to the author of the epic poems *The Iliad* and *The Odyssey*. These works became the standards of Grecian ideals of courage.

Pythagoras (sixth century BC): Philosopher who sought philosophical meanings in the study of mathematics.

Pericles (c. 495-429 BC): Statesman and general who led the democratic golden age of Athens.

Herodotus (c. 484-424 BC): Author of *Histories*, considered the first historian of Western Civilization.

Socrates (c. 469-399 BC): Philosopher who taught through a method of questioning and debate.

Plato (c. 429-347 BC): Student of Socrates who taught the existence of a creator god. He also taught that all things are copies of ideals.

Aristotle (c. 384-322 BC): Philosopher who sought to create rules of logic. He was a student of Plato.

Alexander the Great (356-323 BC): A Macedonian king who absorbed the Greek city states into his empire. He also conquered the Persian Empire, Asia Minor and Egypt, and pushed his army into India.

Zeno (c. 340-265 BC): Founder of the philosophy known as Stoicism.

---

colony in Southern Italy. Pythagoras is best remembered for his mathematical formula known as the Pythagorean Theorem, which states that on a right-angled triangle, the sum of the squares of the two short sides equals the square of the long side.

Pythagoras grew up on the island of Samos, but traveled the Mediterranean with his merchant father. He lived in Egypt, where he studied its religion. After the Persian invasion of Egypt he was carted off to Babylon as a prisoner. There he learned astrology, mathematics, music and "a very mystical worship of the gods."[2] From these experiences he created a philosophy containing elements from both science and the mystery religions.

The ascetic philosophy of the Pythagoreans included belief in the transmigration of souls (reincarnation); that the key to knowledge is contained in mathematics; and that a life of harmony is obtained through contemplation, music and gymnastics. Pythagoreans developed a complex doctrine in the mystic meanings of numbers. They also practiced vegetarianism.[3] In many ways, Pythagoras laid the foundation for future Greek philosophers.

Nearly a century after Pythagoras, Athens and Sparta faced off in the Peloponnesian War. A new philosophy, fueled by war weariness, formed among a generation softened by the prosperity of Athenian sea trade. Adherents began to question the old ideas of absolute good. This new movement taught that virtue was defined by personal desires and feelings. Materialism became the ultimate goal of life. These philosophers, called sophists, believed that all matter was comprised of the smallest of particles, called atoms. The material universe, including human life, was a result of blind chance.[4]

The sophists rejected any objective standards, claiming all cultures and religions were human inventions. The existence of the gods was debated, and some sophists promoted atheism. Since there was no absolute truth, political views, religious beliefs and morality were seen as the subjective concepts of each individual. (The word sophistry in English means an argument based on clever, but unsound reasoning).

One philosopher, named Socrates (c. 460-399 BC), stood against the sophists by arguing for the existence of objective standards of good and evil. Socrates taught that instead of abandoning oneself to passions, human emotions and impulses, the virtuous person controlled his thoughts and emotions through the study of philosophy. By living a virtuous life, and doing good deeds, a person could obtain true happiness. [5]

Socrates might have infuriated the sophists, but he was also a target for the traditional Athenians who resented the way he questioned the political establishment. The Athenian state demanded Socrates denounce his philosophy. When he refused, it demanded his suicide.

In *Phaedo*, Plato recorded the words of Socrates as he discussed his approaching death. Socrates stated that he did not fear death because it is the goal of philosophy to reject material things and prepare the soul for the afterlife. He explained his concept of death as a question: "Is it not the separation of soul and body? And to be dead is the completion of this; when the soul exists in herself, and is released from the body and the body is released from the soul, what is this but death?"[6]

Socrates went on to argue that the closest a human being comes to true knowledge is the moment he is least concerned with the functions of the body. He concluded that true philosophers "are always occupied with the practice of dying."[7]

Socrates left no original writings. His student Plato (c. 427-347 BC) recorded his teacher's ideas in a series of dialogues in which Socrates asks questions and leads others to his conclusions. This technique became known as the Socratic Method.

Plato continued to develop Socrates' ideas. Socrates' student believed in two realms of existence—mind and matter. In the realm of mind, or spirit, there are ideals, or archetypes. Objects in the material realm are copies of the ideals. Plato called the creator god the *demiurge* (craftsman) who was the ideal good. Matter eternally existed in a state of chaos, but the *demiurge* created imperfect objects using the model of ideal objects and perfect forms like beauty, goodness and virtue.

After the *demiurge* made the universe, he created the deities of Mount Olympus, and then the souls of lesser beings. Human souls first inhabited the heavens, but eventually desired to experience the material world, so the lesser gods prepared bodies for them to inhabit. The earth itself was given a soul.[8]

For Plato, the goal of human life was to become virtuous through philosophy and reincarnation, eventually returning to the original divine state. He quoted Socrates in the *Republic*: "Then this must be our notion of the just man, that even when he is in poverty or sickness, or any other seeming misfortune, all things in the end will work together for the good of him in life and death: for the gods have a care for anyone whose desire is to become just and to be like God, as far as a man can attain the divine likeness, by the pursuit of virtue?"[9]

Plato rejected Athenian democracy and espoused a government ruled by a professional aristocracy specially trained for leadership.[10]

The third person in the Greek philosophical triad was Aristotle (c. 384-322 BC), who developed a system of logic and scientific exploration. Aristotle divided philosophy into three categories: mathematics, physics and metaphysics. He further taught that practical philosophy is concerned with ethics and politics while poetic philosophy dealt with emotional reactions to art, poetry and drama.

Aristotle's logic involved gathering facts and deciphering a conclusion. He divided logic into two methods: deduction—drawing a conclusion from the universal to the particular; and induction—drawing a conclusion from the particular to the universal.[11]

Two Greek philosophies, Stoicism and Epicureanism, are mentioned in the biblical book of Acts when the apostle Paul spoke to the philosophers at the Athenian Areopagus.[12]

The Stoics, founded by Zeno (c. 340-265 BC), believed that a good life is based on practicing discipline, living in harmony with nature, and exercising self-control so that reason controls passions. The virtues of self-control, self-efficiency and independence were believed to render a person indifferent to pain or pleasure. Meditation would lead to inner peace. Stoic religion involved the worship of a singular creator god, although Stoics also believed in the existence of various spirits. The Stoic god permeated all creation, but he did not interact with humans on a personal basis.[13]

On the other hand, the Epicureans, followers of Epicurus (c. 341-270 BC), believed that seeking happiness, which was defined as pleasure, resulted in a good life. Anything that made a person happy was considered good. The gods held little relevance to a philosophy in which physical happiness and sensations were the goal of life.[14]

Alexander the Great

In the second half of the fourth century BC, the Macedonians were a diverse group of people living north of Greece. Their ruler, King Philip II, marched through the Greek peninsula. The Hellenic city states finally found themselves united, albeit against their will. In 336 BC, when Greek unity was completed, Philip was murdered. His 20-year-old son Alexander, under the suspicion of having engineered his father's assassination, replaced him.

Many of the Greek city states showed little enthusiasm for Alexander's rule. The animosity between Macedonians and Greeks was so intense that some Greeks refused to participate in Alexander's army of conquest.[15]

Alexander was a student of Aristotle, displayed remarkable military skills, and was driven by ruthless ambition. His Macedonian-Greek army conquered Asia Minor, Egypt, Syria, Babylon and Persia. According to Josephus, while Alexander was on his way to Egypt, he visited the temple in Jerusalem, where priests showed him prophecies in the book of Daniel that predicted a Greek victory over Persia.[16] He pushed his army into India until the threat of mutiny stopped the advance.

Alexander began to adopt Persian ways, including a demand that he be worshipped as divine, something many of his soldiers found repulsive. In 323 BC, Alexander came down with a fever and within a short time he died. He was 33 years old.

His death threw the conquered territories into confusion. Alexander had plundered the Persian Empire, Asia Minor and Egypt. However, other than placing Macedonians in charge of existing governments, he had done little to bring any central organization to the conquered territories. Peter Green in *The Hellenistic Age* sums up Alexander's conquests: "...the expedition was fundamentally disruptive rather than constructive in any unifying sense. It began with an urgent need for booty and ended in megalomania."[17]

Still, Alexander the Great left his mark on every area he conquered. Throughout his empire, Alexander and his successors constructed new cities or modified existing ones to conform to a Greek model. In these cities Greek architecture, religion, athletics and culture were introduced to the population. A number of Greek cities sprang up along the Mediterranean coast of Judea and in Samaria. Alexandria, on the Egyptian coast, would eventually become the home of the ancient world's greatest library until it was burned during the Roman occupation.

After Alexander's death, the empire was divided among his generals. Greece returned to the old ways of competing city states. A general named Seleucus took control of much of the old Persian Empire. Another named Ptolemy, hijacking Alexander's corpse and using it as proof of succession, seized Egypt.

Alexander's demise, and the decline of the Macedonian-Greek Empire, did not mean that Greek culture was retreating. The various Macedonian rulers promoted Greek language and customs in the areas under their control, exposing literate people from diverse cultures to the philosophies of Socrates, Plato, Aristotle and Zeno. One ideal the Macedonian kings failed to spread, since it would undermine their power, was Athenian democracy.

For nearly 300 years the lands conquered by Alexander would be embroiled in warfare between competing Macedonian-Greek dynasties. There would also be regional strife, disputes between cities and incursions by various barbarian tribes. The history of Alexander's successors is one of intrigue, brutality, murder and incest. The rulers at times claimed to be gods, and they practiced power politics that took no prisoners.[18]

Greek Influences on Roman Culture

While the Grecian empire fragmented, a new political energy was growing on another peninsula jutting into the northern Mediterranean. Eventually, a Roman tidal wave washed over the Greeks in a series of second century BC wars. The Romans plundered every piece of Greek art and sculpture they could find, carting their booty off to decorate Italy's temples and villas.[19]

Moses Hadas writes about the effects of Hellenistic culture on Rome in *Imperial Rome:* "Rome's career spanned a millennium; in that time Rome assembled the greatest empire the world had seen. But the size and stability of the Empire are not the sum of Rome's claim to greatness. A more enduring claim lies in Rome's marked genius in nourishing and embellishing the intellectual and cultural achievements of the Greek world that it conquered, and spreading them across Europe. Roman architecture, art, literature and religion—all showing the influence of Greece—bear the unmistakable stamp of Roman power and assurance. Nevertheless, Horace's statement is true: 'Captive Greece took Rome captive.'"[20]

Roman upper class families imported Greek tutors to teach their children. Some Romans sent their young men to Athens to further their education in philosophy, arts and science. C.M. Bowes in *Classical Greece* concludes, "Despite the Romans' confidence in their own imperial mission and their gift for government, they felt, a little uneasily, that there was much in art, letters and thought which they could never hope to do as well as the Greeks."[21] The seeds of Hellenism planted in the Macedonian domains were watered by the wake of the Roman legions.

Greek Influences on Jewish Culture

The Jewish homeland became the battleground for wars between the Seleucid and Ptolemaic kingdoms, with armies sweeping back and forth through the countryside, and each side leaving garrisons to guard the territory. Many Jews found themselves struggling to maintain their distinct Jewish culture while others were attracted to Hellenistic influences.

When the Jews won their independence from the Macedonian kings, they continued to struggle with the influences of Hellenism while desiring to maintain a pure Jewish culture. A collection of Jewish writings from the last two centuries before Jesus, now called the *Apocrypha*, reflects both traditional Jewish and Hellenistic influences. This tension would spawn the rise of sects like the Pharisees and Essenes.

An influential proponent of integrating Greek philosophy with Hebrew Scripture was the first century AD Jewish writer Philo from Alexandria, Egypt. Philo taught an allegorical interpretation of the Hebrew Scriptures and considered Plato "the sweetest of writers."[22] He also wrote of the "excellent doctrines" of the Pythagoreans.[23] His fascination with the spiritual importance of numbers is shown in his commentary *On the Creation*, in which he assigned a meaning to each number of the days of creation. Philo embraced the Greek idea of the immortality of the soul.[24] For Philo there were two deaths: one when the soul left the body, and another "death" occurring as "destruction of virtue and admission of vice."[25]

Uneasy Co-Existence

The Greek philosophers saw themselves as the discoverers of universal truth. The Romans saw themselves as the purveyors of a superior civilization. The Jews saw themselves as the exclusive people of God's covenant and the *Torah*; builders and caretakers of *Yahweh's* only temple; and recipients of the land of Israel by divine right. They believed that it was to a religiously pure Israel that the Anointed King would be sent by *Yahweh* to rule all nations. It was into these opposing worldviews, uneasily existing side-by-side within the Roman Empire, that Christianity grew.

4

THE LEGACY OF
ROMULUS AND REMUS

W hen Julius Caesar marched his legions across the Rubicon River in 49 BC, the Roman Republic was in a state of political decay. Perpetual civil wars had destabilized the government and the Senate's power was waning.

Caesar crushed the armies of his rival Pompey in Spain and Greece. Pompey fled to Egypt, but Caesar was deprived of his final triumph when the young Egyptian-Ptolemaic king presented him with Pompey's head. According to Plutarch, Caesar turned away from the sight in disgust. When presented with Pompey's seal he burst into tears.[1]

Caesar added Ptolemy's sister, Queen Cleopatra, to his conquests before returning to Rome where he reorganized the government, created employment projects for the poor, enacted laws and instituted the Julian calendar. Intent on consolidating power, he had himself declared dictator by the Senate in 46 BC. Many senators resented his meteoric rise to authority, so in 44 BC a group conspired to kill Caesar as he entered the senate building. After Caesar's murder, the empire was divided into three sections. Mark Anthony governed in the East, Octavian in the West and Lepidus in Africa.

Mark Anthony established his headquarters in Egypt, where he fell under Cleopatra's spell. He divorced his Roman wife, who happened to be Octavian's sister. Roman nature being what it was, soon the three rulers were engaged in a bloody civil war. In 31 BC, Octavian defeated Anthony in the battle of Actium. Anthony and Cleopatra committed suicide. Octavian became the sole ruler of a unified empire, taking the title Augustus, or "revered one."[2] The Roman Empire was reaching the age of its greatest power and influence.

Roman Life

The center of the capital city ruled by Augustus was a magnificent collection of government buildings and temples. Residential areas, with large houses surrounding a central courtyard, supplied the rich and middle class a sense of privacy. The Pantheon, with its domed roof, illustrated Roman architectural genius. The Circus Maximus accommodated enormous crowds who watched chariot races and gladiatorial games. Augustus launched new building projects, creating a renewed Imperial Forum.

As the capital of a unified empire, Rome was becoming the largest consumer society in the world. Merchants imported everything from common household utensils to luxury items from all over the empire. Imported food was so inexpensive that the only way many farmers living in the countryside around Rome could turn a profit was to consolidate into large-scale farms utilizing slave labor. This choice forced many small farmers to move into the city in search of economic opportunity, but the ample numbers of slaves created little need for hired labor. In the shadow of Rome's magnificent buildings and thriving prosperity existed high unemployment, poverty and squalor.[3]

Moses Hadas in *Imperial Rome* describes this other Rome: "In the days of Augustus, about a million people lived in Rome, most of them jammed into stuffy, malodorous apartments. (They smelled so bad that Pliny suggesting disguising the odor by burning bread.) People complained about the housing shortage, soaring rents, congested traffic, polluted air, crime in the streets and the high cost of living."[4]

This led to one of Rome's most unique customs—the patron-client relationship. Wealthy men would bestow legal protection and financial assistance to the poor. When unemployed, the poor person could arrive at the house of the patron and receive assistance. In response, the client would give political support and show respect to his patron in public by addressing him as "master."[5] In hard times, the unemployed could quickly turn into a riotous mob and numerous emperors would pacify them with the violent entertainment of gladiatorial games.

At the bottom of Roman society were the slaves. They became so inexpensive that even middle class families could own slaves to do household chores. Entrepreneurs accumulated slaves of various skills so they could rent them out as construction crews or for specialized duties. Slaves had no legal rights and their welfare depended totally on the whims of their owners. Sexual abuse of slaves was common.[6]

The foundation of Roman society was the family. During the Republic, the head of the house legally owned every family member. He could dish out punishment at will, including disowning a child or even legally inflicting the death penalty. By the time of Augustus, social norms had changed so that few fathers would actually carry out their legal right to kill their progeny. Augustus tried to strengthen families and morality through imperial legislation.

In practice, marriage could be for romantic or social reasons, or just as a matter of convenience. Moses Hadas writes, "There were three forms of marriage service, two of which made the wife the legal chattel of her spouse—but that did not keep the wives from exercising a profound influence, even control, over their husbands. It is also worth noting that in this family-oriented society the stigma of illegitimacy was social rather than moral: the unacknowledged child owed loyalty to no family and had no rightful place in his society."[7]

Though marriage was socially important, divorce was acceptable and easy to attain. Roman virtue encouraged familial affection and lifelong marriages, but because of high mortality rates, many times even marriages of devoted couples didn't last more than twenty years.[8]

Since a fetus was considered property, with no moral or legal rights, abortion was common. A newborn wasn't accepted as a human being until it had been picked up by the father and declared legitimate. If the father refused to perform this ceremony, the baby could be legally killed or abandoned. Unwanted babies were abandoned by the roadside where they were left to the elements to die, or to be picked up by someone to adopt or to raise as a slave.[9]

The exposure of female infants was high, as was the rate of early deaths by women in childbirth or through botched abortions. The result of high female mortality produced an abundance of males with little hopes of marriage. It has been estimated that first century Rome contained over one hundred and thirty men for every hundred women.[10] The beneficiary of this imbalance was the Roman army, which had ample supplies of young men to fill the ranks of the legions.

Legal adoption was often practiced among the Roman upper class. This ceremony gave the adopted person the same rights as a biological child. It was not uncommon for wealthy Romans to adopt an adult male who was considered worthy to manage the family wealth and carry on the family name.[11]

Roman children, at least in the wealthier classes, received a formal education. The families who wanted the best education for their children brought Greek tutors into the home for individual instruction.[12]

A familiar routine for many Romans was attendance at the public baths, where men and women sometimes freely mingled together. These bathhouses were places of business and gossip, and they often offered musical performances, games and exercise rooms.[13]

Although Romans generally denounced adultery or incest, both were common. Any sexual activity with a slave was acceptable, as was homosexuality, especially between an older man and a boy.[14]

Important Romans

Romulus and Remus: Mythical twin brothers said to have been saved by a wolf and raised by a shepherd who discovered them. While founding the city of Rome, Romulus killed his brother and named the city after himself.

Cato (234-149 BC): An important senator during the days of the Roman Republic. The Republic disappeared under the dictatorship of Julius Caesar in 44 BC.

Crassus (c. 112-53 BC): Famous soldier who is well known for quelling the slave revolt led by Spartacus.

Cicero (106-43 BC): Influential politician and writer.

Mark Anthony (82-30 BC): Soldier and statesman who is famous for conspiring with the Egyptian Queen Cleopatra and competing with Octavian (Augustus) for power after the death of Julius Caesar.

Virgil (70-19 BC): Well-known Roman poet.

Horace (65-8 BC): Well-known Roman poet.

Livy (59 BC-17 AD): Roman historian.

Ovid (c. 43 BC-18 AD): Well-known Roman poet.

Seneca (c. 5 BC-65 AD): A Stoic philosopher, writer and politician, Seneca was Nero's teacher.

Pliny the Elder (23-79 AD): Writer, politician and soldier. He died while studying the volcanic eruption of Mount Vesuvius.

Pliny the Younger (c. 61-113 AD): The nephew of Pliny the Elder. Governor of a Roman territory. He wrote to Emperor Trajan concerning Christians.

Plutarch (c. 46-120 AD): Biographer who wrote *Lives of the Noble Grecians and Romans.*

Roman Religion

Traditional Roman religion had little to do with the spiritual or moral nature of the participants. It was a religion of ritual and superstition. Gods and goddesses were supernatural beings—as fickle and flawed as any human—who had to be appeased in order for a supplicant to receive help in time of need.[15]

Jupiter, the chief of the gods, was the deity of rain and storms, while his wife, Juno, was the goddess of womanhood. Minerva was the goddess of handicrafts and wisdom; Venus, of sexual love and birth; Vesta, of the hearth and sacred fires; Ceres, of farming and harvests. The Greeks considered Hermes to be the messenger of the gods, but the Romans worshipped Mercury, their equivalent, as the god of trade. Roman businessmen celebrated his feast day to increase profits. Other Roman deities included Mars, the god of war; Castor and Pollux, the gods of sea travelers; Cronos, the guardian of time; and Cupid, the god of love. His arrows inspired humans and immortals to fall in love.

Romans would generically call on "the gods," but each deity had its own cult. Devout worshipers attended religious ceremonies in specific temples, each dedicated to a particular god or goddess. Priests sacrificed animals and studied the entrails for signs from the gods, especially in the color, size and shape of the liver. These ceremonies became elaborate public spectacles in which the common person was only a spectator.

Most people saw themselves as pawns of the gods. Superstitious imploring of the gods permeated every decision and event of life. Astrologists were sought for guidance from the stars and the flights of birds were studied for secret messages—a custom said to have originated with Romulus and Remus who, according to legend, used the flights of birds to determine which of the two would lay out the city of Rome.[16]

The emperor was *pontifex maximus*, or spiritual leader of all Rome. Augustus was declared a god after his death, and Caligula demanded that his subjects worship him while he was still alive. By the time the early Christians were spreading their message across the empire, pagans were showing their loyalty to Rome by sacrificing to the emperor and seeking his divine favor.[17]

Romans readily accepted religions from other lands, so temples to foreign deities sprang up in Rome. Three Eastern cults common in Rome were dedicated to the worship of the Asian goddess Cybele, the Egyptian goddess Isis and the Persian god Mithra. From Rome, these practices were exported throughout the empire.[18]

The Romans showed great interest in Greek philosophies. The one they identified with the most, and adapted to their ideals, was Stoicism. Stoics believed that the universe is composed of four elements—fire, air, water and earth. The universe was created by a lawgiver who designed every aspect of nature. History is an endless cycle through which each age is destroyed by fire and then reborn.

Bertrand Russell in *A History of Western Philosophy* explains the Stoic concept of God: "God is not separate from the world; He is the soul of the world, and each of us contains a part of the Divine Fire. All things are parts of one single system, which is called Nature, the individual life is good when it is in harmony with Nature. In one sense, *every* life is in harmony with Nature, since it is such as Nature's laws have caused it to be; but in another sense a human life is only in harmony with Nature when the individual will is directed to ends which are among those of Nature. *Virtue* consists of a *will* that is in harmony with Nature. The wicked, though perforce they obey God's law, do so involuntarily....[and] are like a dog tied to a cart, and compelled to go wherever it goes."[19]

The purpose of human life for a Stoic was to learn to control all emotions and to seek guidance in reason and virtue. To the Stoic, the greatest achievement in life was to be without passions and to see life's difficulties as opportunities to experience emotional control. Both negative and positive emotions were seen as weaknesses. Anger, sympathy, grief, sexual desire, envy, hatred and friendship were all to be replaced with "holy calm."[20]

Early Stoics believed that human souls survived until the next destruction of the earth by fire, and then returned for the next creation. Others maintained that at death the soul ceased to exist. By the first century BC, some stoics claimed that the souls of the dead hovered around the earth, invisibly awaiting the next conflagration. This led to the idea that evil souls stayed near the earth, while virtuous ones rose to the stars and guided those still alive through the practice of astrology.[21]

Gladiatorial Games and the Roman Army

The Romans are remembered for more than spreading Greek culture. They are memorialized for their own concepts of law and their feats of engineering genius. They are also remembered for exporting the brutality of gladiatorial games. Long before Augustus, arenas were set up for people in Rome to watch slaves or condemned criminals engage in mortal combat with each other or with wild animals. A few gladiators survived long enough to amass fortune and fame, and to become celebrities.

The Circus Maximus supplied a venue for tens of thousands to watch chariot races and spectacles that not only included individual combat, but also featured groups of gladiators battling to the death in violent plays depicting historical Roman army or naval victories. Animals were imported from Europe, Asia and Africa. The desire for blood and gore was so insatiable that entire species of wild animals became extinct. Smaller but still impressive circuses and arenas were constructed all over the empire—wherever people desired blood-and-guts entertainment.

Once Augustus gained power, the weakened Senate no longer represented the ideals of the Republic and the emperor exercised almost absolute power. His word, as long as it was backed by the legions, was enforced. Sometimes, as in the cases of Caligula and Nero, the emperor found that what the army gave it could take away.

The Romans are remembered for their engineering and administrative prowess, but their greatest enterprise was war. Infantry units of highly trained and disciplined soldiers, marching in tight formations and armed with shields, short swords and spears, were more than a match for most enemies. Roman use of cavalry and archers, as well as their genius with siege weapons, made the legions masters of the war of movement and the conquest of walled cities.

Romans took great pride in bringing their civilization to the barbarians, even if it was by the edge of a sword. The ultimate Roman dream was one government creating one overriding system of law and economic trade throughout the world.

Jesus of Nazareth, born during the reign of Augustus, proclaimed a different kingdom. That message would bring him into direct conflict with mighty Rome.

Roman Emperors and the Early Church

Julius Caesar	46-44 BC	Crowned dictator in 46 BC, bringing to an end the Roman Republic, which had existed since 509 BC. Caesar was assassinated in 44 BC, bringing about civil war between Mark Anthony and Octavian. The Jews received special protection from him.
Augustus Caesar	27 BC-14 AD	Defeated the forces of Mark Anthony and Cleopatra, Queen of Egypt, taking the title Augustus. He was emperor when Jesus was born. Augustus continued to show special favor to the Jewish people.
Tiberius	14-37 AD	Emperor when Jesus was crucified.
Caligula	37-41 AD	Depraved emperor killed by his own army.
Claudius	41-54 AD	Placed in power by the army because he was believed to be mentally deficient. He expelled the Jews from Rome (Acts 18:1-2).
Nero	54-68 AD	Depraved emperor who carried out great persecutions on Christians and killed the apostles Peter and Paul.

Galba	68-69 AD	
Ortho, Vitelius	69 AD	
Vespasian	69-79 AD	Led war against the Jews.
Titus	79-81 AD	Destroyed Jerusalem in 70 AD as a general. Later became emperor.
Domitian	81-96 AD	Intensely persecuted Christians.
Nerva	96-98 AD	
Trajan	98-117 AD	Persecuted Christians.
Hadrian	117-138 AD	Persecuted Christians.
Antonius Pius	138-161 AD	Persecuted Christians.
Marcus Aurelius	161-180 AD	Persecuted Christians. A Stoic philosopher.

There were numerous emperors between 180 and 306 when Constantine started his rise to power. He became the emperor over the Western Empire in 312 and ruled over both the East and the West from 324 to 337.

5

A RABBI NAMED JESUS

Jesus of Nazareth was a Jew born into a society in which every aspect of daily life was dominated by a belief that its shared religion and customs separated the Jews as the special people of the only God. The *Torah* regulated the ebb and flow of weekly Sabbath rituals, the proper food served at meals, marriage customs, family life and the rejection of any association with idols. The center of the Jewish world was Herod's magnificent temple in Jerusalem.

Throughout Judea the influences of Greece and Rome were apparent in the architecture of a gymnasium or amphitheater or in the legionnaires strolling through the marketplace. Herod's port city of Caesarea was a testimony to Roman engineering. Situated on an area of the Mediterranean shore not suited for a harbor, the port was constructed by creating a breakwater using concrete blocks weighing as much as 50 tons. The city was laid out on a Roman grid design and included a large amphitheater, a hippodrome, public baths, temples, government offices,

warehouses and offices. Josephus wrote, "It was of excellent
workmanship; and this was the more remarkable for being built in
a place that of itself was not suitable to such noble structures, but
was to be brought to perfection by materials from other places,
and at very great expense."[1]

It was during Herod's reign that Jesus was born. Later, Jesus'
followers claimed his miraculous virgin birth was the fulfillment
of a prophetic promise of the Messiah. He was circumcised on the
eighth day and raised in a *Torah*-observant family. His knowledge
of Hebrew Scripture was so complete that by the time he reached
age 12, he was astounding the temple teachers.[2] Jesus spent his
young manhood working as a carpenter.[3]

Around age 30 Jesus came to his cousin, an unconventional
holy man known as John the Baptist, to receive ritual water
baptism. John was from a priestly family and known throughout
Judea as a controversial prophet who claimed that the Jewish
people had strayed from God, and he called for them to repent
and return to the true worship of *Yahweh*.[4]

After his baptism, Jesus launched his own ministry and was
soon as controversial as his cousin. His debates with religious
leaders reflect common themes in first century Judaism—how
to observe the Sabbath, how to interpret the *Torah* and how to
worship the God of Israel properly.

In the Sermon on the Mount Jesus made startling claims that it
was through his teachings that a person could understand the true
nature of the *Torah*. He claimed that not one of the smallest letters
or strokes of the pen in the law would "pass away" until "all is
fulfilled." Jesus explained that while the rabbis taught the letter of
the law, he brought a more complete understanding. He declared
that morality encompasses more than the actual act of murder
and must involve rejecting hatred. The rabbis taught that adultery
is a sin. Jesus claimed that lusting for a woman in the mind, even
if it doesn't lead to the act of adultery, is sin.

He taught people how to pray and how not to be anxious about their physical needs. He taught that the core meaning of the Law and the Prophets is "whatever you want men to do to you, do also to them." One of the harshest teachings in the Sermon on the Mount is that in the Day of Judgment Jesus will reject many of those who claim to be his followers because they "practice lawlessness."[5]

His teachings appealed to common folk, while many of the religious leaders found him baffling. As Jesus' followers grew in numbers, so did his attacks on the religious elite. The groups who received the most scathing criticism were the Pharisees and Sadducees.

The Pharisees

During the four centuries between Malachi, the last of the Old Testament prophets, and John the Baptist, Judea was ruled by the Persians, the Ptolemies of Egypt and the Seleucids of Syria, then gained independence under the leadership of the Jewish Maccabaeus family only to fall under the Roman sandal. By the time of Jesus, the Sanhedrin, a ruling council comprised of priests, scribes and nobles, regulated Jerusalem's daily political and religious life under the watchful eye of the Roman governor.

In the second century BC, Antiochus IV, also known as Epiphanes, "the manifest god," invaded Judea. The result was the brutal oppression of the Jews by the Seleucid king. Antiochus, a worshipper of the Greek pantheon, issued an edict that his entire realm convert to one religion. He forbade, upon penalty of death, the observance of the Sabbath, circumcision and the Jewish food laws. He went as far as to kill mothers who had their babies circumcised. A statue of Zeus was set up in the temple, Jews were forced to participate in pagan worship rituals, and anyone found with a copy of the *Torah* was executed. [6]

In 167 BC the Jews revolted under the leadership of the Maccabaeus family, gaining independence in 141 BC. The exile to

Babylon, return to the Promised Land, oppression by Antiochus IV and independence under the Maccabees created a fire in the hearts of many Jews never again to be estranged from God and driven from their homeland. Their history, their very existence as a people, was inexorably linked to their covenant relationship with *Yahweh*. That relationship was maintained through the study of the *Torah*, temple worship and the land of Israel itself, for it was to this land the Messiah was prophesied to come.

During the second century BC the Hasidaeans, or "pious ones," organized to protect the religion of the covenant from Greek and pagan influences as "each one [was] a volunteer on the side of the Law."[7] The Hasidaeans, zealous in their desire never again to allow the desecration of Israel, were the predecessors of the Pharisees and the Essenes.

The name Pharisee is derived from an Aramaic word *peras* meaning "to separate."[8]

The Pharisees, who were well entrenched in Jewish society by the last decades of the second century BC, comprised a new concept in the structure of Judaism. Many non-priest scribes became Pharisees. The interpretation of the *Torah* was traditionally a priestly duty and the priests gravitated to a party known as the Sadducees.[9] Conflicts between a party that was predominantly non-priests, and the priestly Sadducees, were inevitable.

Judea would again feel the conquerors heel with the Roman invasion in 63 BC. Eventually, the Romans crowned the Herodian family as rulers over the region. There were constant political and religious conflicts among the Herodians, Romans, Sanhedrin, Zealots, Pharisees, Sadducees and other factions.

Josephus recorded that the Pharisees "valued themselves highly upon the exact skill of the law of their fathers, and made men believe that they were highly favored by God."[10]

The Pharisees created an elaborate system of oral laws designed to protect the *Torah* from defilement. They were so consumed with traditions and ritual purity that one rabbi claimed, "It is a tradition among the Pharisees to torment themselves in this world, and yet they will gain nothing by it in the next." Others accused, "the Pharisees would by-and-by subject the globe of the sun to their purifications."[11]

The major traits of the Pharisees were:

- Strict adherence to the law.

- Holding that the oral law was as authoritative as the written *Torah*.

- Strong hope in a Messiah to come and establish Israel as God's chosen people.

- Belief in the resurrection of the dead. Josephus claimed that they believed in the immortality of the soul and that the souls of evil men received eternal punishment while the souls of good men were resurrected into a new body.[12]

- A highly developed system of belief in angels.[13]

Jesus and Oral Tradition

A group of Pharisees reproached Jesus and accused his disciples of not participating in ritual hand washing before eating. This oral ritual was based in the belief that a dinner table was a type of altar, and the man of the house a priest of his own home, so he should follow the priestly ritual of washing before presenting a sacrifice by washing before eating.[14]

Jesus answered his antagonists with the question, "Why do you also transgress the commandment of God because of your tradition?" He then condemned the *Corban* vow. This oral tradition allowed someone to dedicate his wealth to the temple but continue to use it until death. The participant could then deny supporting his parents by claiming his wealth belonged to God. Jesus denounced this tradition as an attempt to negate God's commandment to honor mother and father.[15]

After showing how the *Corban* vow actually violated one of the Ten Commandments, Jesus dealt with ritual hand washing. "Do you not yet understand," he said to his disciples, "that whatever enters the mouth goes into the stomach and is eliminated? For out of the heart proceed evil thoughts, murders, adulteries, fornications, thefts, false witness, blasphemies. These are the things which defile a man, but to eat with unwashed hands does not defile a man."

Jesus supported the written *Torah* and expounded its underlying principles while condemning many oral traditions as attempts to sidestep God's intent. He taught that a person's moral thoughts, motivations and obedience to God's law are more important than the minuscule rituals designed to "hedge" the law. Jesus claimed many times these rituals led to the misapplication of the laws they were supposed to protect.

On another occasion, some Pharisees challenged Jesus concerning the legality of healing on the Sabbath. Jesus asked them, "What man is there among you who has one sheep, and if it falls into a pit on the Sabbath, will not lay hold of it and lift it out? Of how much more value then is a man than a sheep? Therefore it is lawful to do good on the Sabbath." The logic of his reply silenced the Pharisees, fanning hatred in some to conspire to kill him.[16]

(The Essenes had a stricter interpretation of the sheep in the ditch scenario. A *Dead Sea Scroll* fragment states that if a cow falls into water on the Sabbath a person may not help it, but if a man falls into the water a person may throw him his garment to lift him out of harm's way.[17])

The Jewish Sabbath was hedged with a bewildering array of oral regulations. Since the Sabbath commandment forbids work on that day, the rabbis created 39 categories of work.

Sabbath rules stated that rainwater could be collected and carried for immediate use, but it was sin to carry rainwater if it ran down a wall. There were debates over the lawfulness of throwing something in the air and catching it with the opposite hand. One argument held that it was only lawful to catch it with your mouth and eat it. It was considered a burden to lift anything that weighed more than a dried fig.

The schools of Hillel and Shammai engaged in endless disputes on issues such as whether a person could send a letter on Wednesday, Thursday or Friday since the post still might be carried on the Sabbath. The school of Shammai decided that on the Sabbath cold water could be poured on hot water, but not hot on cold. There were meticulous instructions on how to dress. A woman was forbidden to look into a mirror because she might be tempted to pull out a stray hair. A radish could be dipped in salt, but only for a very short time since leaving it there longer would begin the pickling process.[18]

Throughout his ministry Jesus was confronted by Pharisees concerning oral Sabbath traditions. His response was to defend what he claimed was God's original intent for the Sabbath and the law given to the people of Israel.

Jesus' most scathing criticism of this religious group was that many were hypocrites. He accused them of binding difficult regulations on others while considering themselves above the law. He claimed that "all their works they do to be seen of men" and that they were meticulous in tithing but "neglected the weightier matters of the law: justice and mercy and faith." Jesus went as far as to call the Pharisees "whitewashed tombs which indeed appear beautiful outwardly, but inside are full of dead men's bones and all uncleanness." [19]

Teachings of Jesus the Rabbi
in the Gospel of Matthew

"Blessed are the poor in spirit, for theirs is the kingdom of heaven.

Blessed are those who mourn, for they shall be comforted.

Blessed are the meek, for they shall inherit the earth.

Blessed are those who hunger and thirst for righteousness, for they shall be filled.

Blessed are the merciful, for they shall obtain mercy.

Blessed are the pure in heart, for they shall see God.

Blessed are the peacemakers, for they shall be called sons of God.

Blessed are those who are persecuted for righteousness' sake, for theirs is the kingdom of heaven." [20]

"Judge not, that you be not judged. For with what judgment you judge, you will be judged..." [21]

"Not everyone who says to Me, 'Lord, Lord' shall enter into the kingdom of heaven, but he who does the will of My Father in heaven. Many will say to Me in that day, 'Lord, Lord, have we not prophesied in your name, and done many wonders in your name?' And I will declare to them, 'I never knew you; depart from Me, you who practice lawlessness.'" [22]

"Therefore whoever confesses Me before men, him will I also confess before my Father who is in heaven. But whoever denies me before men, him will I also deny before My Father who is in heaven. Do not think that I came to bring peace on earth. I did not come to bring peace but a sword. For I have come to set a man against his father, a daughter against her mother, and a daughter-in-law against her mother-in-law; and a man's enemies will be those of his own household." [23]

"Assuredly, I say to you, unless you are converted and become as little children, you will by no means enter the kingdom of God." [24]

"If your hand or foot causes you to sin, cut it off and cast it from you. It is better for you to enter into life lame or maimed, rather than having two hands or two feet, to be cast into everlasting fire." [25]

When asked by Peter if he should forgive someone who had harmed him seven times, Jesus answered, "I do not say to you, up to seven times, but up to seventy times seven." [26]

"And I say to you, whoever divorces his wife, except for sexual immorality, and marries another, commits adultery; and whoever marries her who is divorced commits adultery." [27]

A man came to Jesus asking how to obtain eternal life. Jesus answered, "...if you want to enter into life, keep the commandments." The man asked, "Which ones?" Jesus answered, "'You shall not murder,' 'You shall not commit adultery,' 'You shall not steal,' 'You shall not bear false witness,' 'Honor your father and your mother,' and 'You shall love your neighbor as yourself.'" [28]

"Assuredly, I say to you that it is hard for a rich man to enter the kingdom of heaven. And again I say to you, it is easier for a camel to go through the eye of a needle than for a rich man to enter the kingdom of God." [29]

"And whoever desires to be first among you, let him be your slave—just as the Son of Man did not come to be served, but to serve, and to give His life as a ransom for many." [30]

A man asked Jesus, "Teacher, which is the greatest commandment in the law?" Jesus answered, "'You shall love the LORD your God with all your heart, with all your soul, and with all your mind.' This is the first and great commandment. And the second is like it: 'You shall love your neighbor as yourself.' On these two commandments hang all the Law and the Prophets." [31]

The Sadducees

Tradition claims that the Sadducees derived their name from Zadok, who was the high priest at the time of Kings David and Solomon. The party appeared around the time of the Maccabean revolt under pressure to preserve the priestly caste. The teachings of the Sadducees are difficult to ascertain because they left no original writings. [32]

The reported major beliefs of Sadducees were:

- The *Torah* or Law alone was canonical and the Writings and Prophets were considered secondary writings.

- They reserved the right of priestly interpretation of the *Torah* and disagreed with many oral traditions and Scriptural interpretations of the Pharisees. The Sadducees gained support among the wealthy class. Josephus claims that popular opinion among the commoners often sided with the Pharisees. [33]

- They disagreed with the Pharisees on the resurrection of the dead. [34]

- They denied the existence of spirits or angels. [35]

- They believed in the total free will of man. [36]

Some Sadducees wanted to trap Jesus with a clever argument concerning the resurrection of the dead. The scenario involved seven brothers. One brother married a wife and died. The second brother married her and then he died. Eventually, all seven brothers married the same woman and all of them died. The dilemma was, "Therefore, in the resurrection, whose wife of the seven will she be? For they all had her."

Jesus answered, "You are mistaken, not knowing the Scriptures nor the power of God. For in the resurrection they neither marry nor are given in marriage, but are like angels of God in heaven. But concerning the resurrection of the dead, have you not read what was spoken to you by God, saying, 'I am the God of Abraham, the

God of Isaac, and the God of Jacob?' God is not the God of the dead, but of the living."

Jesus argued that marriage is an institution of the present age, but the resurrection is to life in a future age. Those resurrected in the future age will be immortal spirit beings, and like angels, won't procreate. Here Jesus defends his resurrection doctrine with such clarity that Luke adds that some of the scribes answered, "Teacher, you have spoken well." [37]

The Sadducees found Jesus as baffling as the Pharisees did. The popularity of Jesus presented a threat to the prestige and power of the priestly and aristocratic Sadducees. There was little room in their perspective, or in the Pharisaical Messianic vision, for a carpenter from Galilee who spent more time deriding them for their faults than denouncing the Romans and setting up the Kingdom of God on earth.

The Essenes

The Essenes were the strictest of first century Jewish religious groups. They accepted marriage as necessary for procreation, but eschewed it themselves in the pursuit of a higher spirituality found in the avoidance of pleasure. The Essenes rejected individual wealth and shared possessions among themselves. They performed intricate purity rituals and wore nothing but white garments.

Josephus claims that they adopted the Greek concept of the afterlife by believing that human souls had been enticed into the prison of their physical bodies. Upon death good souls inhabited a peaceful region beyond the ocean while bad souls went to a place of eternal punishment. [38]

Like the Pharisees, the Essenes expected the Messiah to exalt Israel and rule over all the earth. [39]

Hillel

Hillel (c.60 BC-20 AD) is considered one of the greatest of all rabbinical teachers. He was born in Babylon and migrated to Judea in order to further his studies. He became famous for his teachings, including seven rules for study of the *Torah* and development of *halakhah*. Some of his famous sayings include:

"Be among the disciples of Aaron, loving peace, cherishing mankind, and bringing people closer to the Law."

"He who advertises his name, loses it; he who does not increase knowledge, diminishes it; he who refuses to learn, merits extinction; and he who puts his talent to selfish use, commits spiritual suicide."

"...don't condemn your comrade until you are in his place; and... don't say 'I shall study when I find time,' because you may never find it." [40]

When asked by a man to teach him the entire law while he stood on one foot Hillel answered, "What is hateful to you do not do to your fellow: that is the whole Law; all the rest is its interpretation. Go and learn!" [41]

6

THE JEWISH MESSIAH

Jesus stood before the congregation in a synagogue in Nazareth. He opened the scroll of Isaiah and read: "The Spirit of the LORD is upon Me, because He has anointed Me to preach the gospel to the poor; He has sent Me to heal the brokenhearted, to proclaim liberty to the captives and recovery of sight to the blind, to set at liberty those who are oppressed; to proclaim the acceptable year of the LORD."

The man who made his living as a carpenter then declared to the astonished crowd, "Today this Scripture is fulfilled in your hearing." They responded by attempting to murder him.[1]

Jesus launched his ministry by traveling throughout Galilee performing miraculous healings. Soon throngs of people came to hear his words and to witness the miracles. Wherever he went, his core message was, "Repent, for the kingdom of heaven is at hand."[2]

People were confused about the mission and role of Jesus in fulfilling God's plan for Israel. Some individuals concluded that he was the resurrection of his famous cousin, John the Baptist, whom Herod had killed; others thought he was Elijah, Jeremiah or one of the other Old Testament prophets.[3]

The Apostle John's account of the life and teachings of Jesus supplies many unique details absent in the other gospels. John emphasized Jesus as the prophesied Jewish Messiah, or Christ (from the Greek *Christos*), and his relationship to the future resurrection. He records an encounter between Jesus and a woman named Martha, whose brother Lazarus had died.

"Jesus said to her, 'I am the resurrection and the life. He who believes in me, though he may die, he shall live. And whoever lives and believes in Me shall never die. Do you believe this?'"

"She said to Him, 'Yes Lord, I believe you are the Christ, the Son of God, who is to come into the world.'" Jesus then performed one of his greatest miracles by raising Lazarus from the dead.[4]

On another occasion, Jesus accused some people of following his ministry only because they wanted to see miracles. Jesus claimed that he was the "bread of life" and that those who follow him would receive eternal life at the resurrection of the "last day."

He then made this startling statement: "I am the living bread which came down from heaven. If anyone eats of this bread, he will live forever; and the bread I shall give is My flesh, which I shall give for the life of the world." Jesus also claimed that he was going to return to heaven, where he had been before coming into the world. Many disciples were so confused and offended by this teaching that they left him. When he asked the 12 disciples of his inner circle whether they were also going to leave him, Peter replied that they believed that he was the "Christ, the Son of the living God."[5]

In the Hebrew Scriptures God's "anointed" refers to rulers or prophets chosen to fulfill a special role in the divine plan. The Scriptures also contain prophecies of a specific "Anointed One," or Messiah, who would be a future supreme King. He would restore Israel to greatness and rule the earth from Jerusalem.[6]

During the century before Jesus, the Jews fervently longed for the Messiah to save Israel from their oppressors. The *Jewish Encyclopedia* states: "Not until after the fall of the Maccabean dynasty, when the despotic government of Herod the Great and his family, and the increasing tyranny of the Roman empire had made their condition ever more unbearable, did the Jews seek refuge in the hope of a personal Messiah. They yearned for the promised deliverer of the house of David, who would free them from the yoke of the hated foreign usurper, would put an end to the impious Roman rule, and would establish His own reign of peace and justice in its place. In this way their hopes became gradually centered in the coming of the Messiah."[7]

The *Dead Sea Scrolls* contain predictions of a Messianic kingdom. *The Messiah of Heaven and Earth* stated, "The Heavens and the earth will obey His Messiah and all that is in them. He will not turn aside from the commandments of the Holy Ones." The scroll goes on to declare that the Messiah will "heal the sick, resurrect the dead, and to the meek announce glad tidings...."[8] Both Josephus and Tacitus wrote that a reason many Jews revolted against the Romans in 66 AD was that they anticipated a Jewish king who would rule the entire earth.[9]

The intensity of Messianic anticipation is illustrated in an incident recorded in the Gospel of Luke. Joseph and Mary brought the baby Jesus to the temple to complete the dedication ritual. A man named Simeon, "waiting for the Consolation of Israel," claimed that God had revealed, "he would not see death before he had seen the Lord's Christ." When Simeon saw Jesus, he took him into his arms and declared that the child was the fulfillment of Isaiah's Messianic proclamation. [10]

Jesus of Nazareth—thought by many to be the prophesied Messiah of the Hebrew Scriptures—was born in a barn. He was forced to live his early years in a foreign land, then grew up in Galilee with accusations of being illegitimate. He then labored as a simple carpenter before spending his early 30s traveling through Galilee, Judea and Samaria as an itinerant preacher. His short three-and-a-half year ministry brought him into conflict with Jewish religious leaders who considered him anathema and Roman government officials who could accept no kingdom other than Rome.

Jesus' Kingdom Parables

Matthew 13:3-23; Mark 4:4-29; Luke 8:5-15	The Seed and Soil
Mathew 13:24-30	The Wheat and Tares
Matthew 13:31-32; Mark 4:30-32; Luke 13:18-19	The Mustard Seed
Mathew 13:33; Luke 13:20-21	The Leaven
Matthew 13:44	The Treasure in the Field
Matthew 13:45-46	The Pearl of Great Price
Matthew 13:47-50	The Fishing Net
Matthew 22:1-14	The Wedding Feast
Mathew 24:45-51; Luke 12:42-48	The Wise and Faithful Servants
Matthew 25:1-13	The Ten Virgins
Matthew 25:14-30	The Talents
Matthew 25:31-46	The Sheep and Goats
Mark 4:26-29	The Wheat
Mark 13:32-37	The Owner of the House

The Coming Messianic Kingdom in the Olivet Prophecy

Toward the end of his ministry, Jesus took his disciples to the Mount of Olives, where they asked him about "the sign of Your coming, and the end of the age."[11] The disciples anticipated the fulfillment of the Old Testament predictions of God's Anointed ruling over humanity from Jerusalem. Jesus' response is commonly called the Olivet Prophecy.

Jesus predicted that the present age will culminate with many teachers coming in his name, but teaching false religion. There will be "wars and rumors of wars...famines, pestilences, and earthquakes in various places." In spite of persecution of the true followers of Jesus, and humanity living in a spirit of lawlessness, the "gospel of the kingdom" will be preached throughout the world. [12]

These conditions will not happen around only Jerusalem, but will extend over the entire world. Jesus claimed, "For there shall be great tribulation, such as has not been since the beginning of the world, until this time, no, nor ever shall be. And unless those days were shortened, no flesh would be saved; but for the elects' sake those days will be shortened."[13]

Jesus said that his return will be a spectacular event witnessed by all humanity: "Immediately after the tribulation of those days the sun will be darkened, and the moon will not give its light; the stars will fall from heaven, and the powers of the heaven will be shaken. The sign of the Son of Man will appear in heaven, and then all the tribes of the earth will mourn, and they will see the Son of Man coming on the clouds of heaven with power and great glory."[14]

In the Gospel of Matthew, Jesus completed the Olivet Prophecy with three parables explaining the coming "kingdom of heaven." The first parable told of 10 virgins who wait for a bridegroom. It is night and they all have oil lamps. The bridegroom delays and the virgins fall asleep, only to wake to the shout that the bridegroom is approaching. Five of the virgins are running out of oil and must go buy more. The bridegroom arrives and the five who have oil in their lamps join him in the wedding, but the five without oil are locked outside. In this parable Jesus warns his disciples to be spiritually prepared for his return.[15]

In the second parable about the "kingdom of heaven," a rich man travels to a "far country," but first gives three servants talents (a measurement of money). One servant receives five, another receives two, and the last receives one. When the rich man returns he rewards or punishes each servant in relation to how that servant invested his master's talents.[16] Jesus teaches that his disciples will be judged by the measure of what God gives them in their lives.

The third parable is more direct and begins with, "When the son of Man comes in His glory, and all the holy angels with Him, then He will sit on the throne of His glory." In this parable, Jesus divides the people of all nations into sheep and goats. The sheep are those who loved their neighbors and are invited into the Kingdom of God, while the goats are those who hated their neighbors and are given eternal punishment. [17]

In the Olivet Prophecy Jesus revealed to his disciples that he was not going to set up a kingdom on earth at that time. Instead, he explained that he was going to leave, then return later to establish the literal Kingdom of God and to judge mankind. Before Christ's Second Coming, humanity will be living through a time so terrible that if he did not return, all human life would be extinguished.

The Passover: Instituting the New Covenant

Each year, on the 10th day of the first month of the Hebrew calendar, Jewish families selected an unblemished lamb and kept it until the 14th. It was then killed and eaten in a meal commemorating God's intervention on behalf of Israel to save them from Egyptian slavery, and to make them his special people.

Did Jesus Teach that the Kingdom of God is in Your Heart?

Some Pharisees came to Jesus and asked when the kingdom of God would arrive. Jesus answered, "The kingdom of God does not come with observation; nor will they say, 'See here!' or 'See there!' For indeed the kingdom of God is within you."[18]

Some readers have interpreted this passage to mean that Jesus was teaching that the kingdom of God is not a literal kingdom, but that it exists in the hearts of human beings. However, it is inconceivable that Jesus would be saying the Pharisees, his opponents, had the kingdom of God in their hearts. This verse is better translated "the kingdom of God is in the midst" or "among you." Jesus was telling the Pharisees that they were denying the King of the kingdom even as he was among them. [19]

Children and adults rehearsed the story of how their ancestors were slaves in Egypt and how the God of Abraham, Isaac and Jacob sent Moses to lead them to the Promised Land. God caused nine terrible plagues that rained death and destruction on the land and people of Egypt. He then pronounced a 10th plague: he was going to kill all the Egyptian firstborn. The Israelites would be saved if they took the blood of a lamb and put it on their doorposts. The Lord would then "pass over" them. [20]

On the night before his crucifixion, Jesus sat at a Passover meal with his closest disciples, broke bread, and told them, "Take, eat; this is My body." He then passed around a cup of wine and said, "Drink from it, all of you. For this is My blood of the new covenant, which is shed for the remission of sins."[21]

Centuries before, the prophet Jeremiah predicted this new covenant when he wrote, "Behold the days are coming, says the LORD, when I will make a new covenant with the house of Israel and the house of Judah—not according to the covenant I made with their fathers in the day that I took them by the hand to lead them out of the land of Egypt, my covenant which they broke, though I was a husband to them, says the LORD."

"But this is the covenant that I will make with the house of Israel after those days, says the LORD: I will put my law in their minds, and write it on their hearts; and I will be their God, and they shall be my people."[22]

Jesus linked the celebration of the Passover and his sacrificial death with the institution of the prophesied new covenant. This set the stage for Jesus' followers to discover far reaching meanings for all humanity in many of the rituals and symbols of Judaism. [23] Jesus as the Passover Lamb, whose blood and beaten body paid the price for our sins, removed the death penalty required by God's Law. Christians celebrate this substitutionary sacrifice by the symbols of wine and unleavened bread. The unleavened bread of the Days of Unleavened Bread became an important symbol of Jesus as the "living bread."[24] The temple sacrificial system became symbolic of Christ's sacrificial work. The resurrected Jesus now served as a heavenly High Priest.[25]

When the Jesus sect expanded beyond the Judean borders, they didn't observe many of the *Torah's* rituals in the same manner as the Jews, but that didn't mean they rejected those rituals as being meaningless. Instead, they saw the rituals as types of a greater reality revealed in Jesus Christ. They continued to observe Old Testament ceremonies such as the Passover, but with a new understanding.

The Crucifixion and Resurrection

There is no Christianity without the life, death and resurrection of Jesus as the prophesied Jewish Messiah. After the Passover celebration, Jesus and his disciples went to the Garden of Gethsemane, where he struggled with the knowledge of his coming ordeal. There, one of his disciples, named Judas, betrayed him to the Jewish authorities.

Throughout the long night and the next day, Jesus was accused by the Sanhedrin, beaten by soldiers, taken to Herod Antipas the king of Galilee, and eventually condemned to scourging by the Romans. The Roman governor, Pontius Pilate, offered the Jewish crowd a choice of prisoners on whom he would bestow amnesty: They had to choose between Jesus or a political agitator named Barabbas. The people chose the criminal. Jesus was condemned to death by crucifixion.[26]

A central belief of early Christians was that three days and nights after his crucifixion Jesus rose from the dead. The gospels claim that hundreds of people interacted with the resurrected Jesus. Their conviction of the resurrection was so strong that many of them faced persecution and death without wavering in this belief.

Jesus' First Followers

The most remarkable aspect of the 12 Jewish men Jesus chose as his inner circle of disciples was that they were so unremarkable. Five were fishermen, one a tax collector, one a Zealot. Not one of them was a religious leader or philosopher. The women who followed him were also common people. At the end of his three-and-a-half year ministry, Jesus had only about 120 dedicated followers.[27]

Soon after Jesus' resurrection, his disciples gathered to observe the annual holy day of Pentecost. Miraculous tongues of fire descended on the worshippers and they began to speak in different languages.[28] These followers soon convinced other Jews that Jesus of Nazareth was the prophesied Messiah. A short time after the events of Pentecost, 3,000 converts were baptized in one day.[29]

There was nothing in the teachings of Jesus of Nazareth that led his followers to believe he had created a new religion. They continued to worship at the Jerusalem temple and to observe the Torah. They were seen by both Jews and outsiders as a Jewish sect. This perception didn't change, even when non-Jews began to respond to their message.[30]

The resurrected Jesus returned to give his disciples instructions to preach his message throughout the world.[31] A daunting task for a small group with no political power or physical resources, but one they would fulfill like few other religious movements in history.

What Did Jesus Look Like?

Experts in forensic anthropology have attempted to determine what Jesus of Nazareth looked like. Mike Fillon, in What Did Jesus Look Like?, writes: "Using methods similar to those police have developed to solve crimes, British scientists, assisted by Israeli archeologists, have recreated what they believe is the most accurate image of the most famous face in history."

The conclusions of this group of scientists stunned many who accepted the traditional idea of Jesus' appearance. "From the time Christian children settle into Sunday school classrooms, an image of Jesus Christ is etched into their minds. In North America he is most often depicted as being taller than his disciples, lean, with flowing, light brown hair, fair skin with light-colored eyes. Familiar though this image may be, it is inherently flawed. A person with these features and physical bearing would have looked very different from everyone else in the region where Jesus lived and ministered."

"From analysis of skeletal remains, archeologists had firmly established that the average build of a Semite male at the time of Jesus was 5 ft. 1 in., with an average weight of 110 pounds. Since Jesus worked outdoors as a carpenter until he was about 30 years old, it is reasonable to assume he was more muscular and physically fit than westernized portraits suggest."[32]

Although it is impossible to determine what Jesus actually looked like, the gospels record that Jesus avoided angry mobs simply by mingling with the crowd, and the traitorous Judas had to identify him with a kiss of betrayal.[33] These incidents indicate that Jesus looked like any other Jew of His day.

The prevalent view of Jesus with flowing locks is also an inaccurate portrayal. It is difficult to imagine that the Apostle Paul would write in 1 Corinthians that it's a shame for a man to have long hair if the Messiah he proclaimed wore his hair long.[34]

Where did the idea of Jesus with long hair originate? For centuries, some have believed that Jesus was under a Nazirite vow. According to the *Torah*, a person taking a Nazirite vow pledged to abstain from wine and grapes, to avoid touching a dead body, and to refrain from cutting his hair until the end of the vow's duration.[35] But the Bible doesn't state that Jesus was a Nazirite.

This misconception is based in part on biblical passages like Matthew 2:23: "And he came and dwelt in a city called Nazareth, that it might be fulfilled which was spoken by the prophets, 'He shall be called a Nazarene.'" Jesus was a Nazarene from Nazareth, not a Nazirite under a vow not to cut his hair.

Old Testament Prophecies
Jesus' Followers Applied to Him as the Messiah

OT PROPHECY	QUOTED IN THE NT
Genesis 12:1-3; 22:16-18: Promise that through Abraham's seed all nations would be blessed.	Luke 1:46-55: Words of Mary, mother of Jesus, claiming that the child within her was a fulfillment of the promise made to Abraham.
Deuteronomy 18:15-19: Moses declares a coming Prophet.	Acts 3:12-26
Psalm 2:1-12: The Messiah to be the Son of God.	Acts 4:24-28
Psalm 22: Written by David about the anguish in his life.	The followers of Jesus also saw Psalm 22 as a prophecy of the suffering Messiah.
Psalm 22:1-5	Mark 15:33-41: Christ quotes these verses as he is dying.
Psalm 22:6-8	Matthew 27:39-44: The Messiah mocked for not saving himself.
Psalm 22:9-17	Matthew 27:26-28: Christ beaten and crucified.
Psalm 22:18	Matthew 27:35: Enemies gambled for his clothing.

OT PROPHECY	QUOTED IN THE NT
Psalm 34:19-20: None of the Messiah's bones would be broken.	John 19:32-36
Psalm 68:18: The Messiah will ascend into heaven.	Ephesians 4:7-10
Psalm 69:9: The Messiah to be overcome with zeal.	John 2:13-17
Isaiah 7:14-16: A virgin to bear a child. ("Immanuel" means "God with us.")	Matthew 1:18-25
Isaiah 11:1-5, 10: A descendant of Jesse, father of King David, to open the door of salvation to the Gentiles.	Acts 13:22-23; Romans 15:8-12
Isaiah 42:1-4; 49:1-7: The Messiah's message to go to all peoples.	Matthew 12:14-21
Isaiah 61:1-3: The Messiah is to bring a message of "good news."	Luke 4:16-21
Malachi 3:1: Promise of a messenger to prepare the way for the Messiah.	Luke 1:5-25 (67-80); Luke 7:24-28: Applied to John the Baptist.

7

GROWTH OF THE JESUS SECT

ifty days after the temple wave-sheaf ceremony during the Feast of Unleavened Bread, devout Jews gathered to observe the Feast of Weeks, also called Pentecost. Around 9:00 a.m. a sound of rushing wind caught the temple crowd's attention. What looked like "tongues of fire" shot down from above onto the heads of some of the worshippers. Those struck by this fire didn't seem harmed. Instead, they began to speak in different languages.

Peter, the same disciple who had denied Jesus a few weeks earlier, addressed the perplexed crowd. He told them that this event was God pouring out his Spirit on human beings as prophesied by the Hebrew prophet Joel. He explained that Jesus was the prophesied Messiah whom they had turned over to the Romans to crucify, but that God had raised him from the dead.

Many in the crowd had heard Jesus and seen his miracles. They were "cut in the heart" and asked Peter and the other followers of Jesus, "what shall we do?"[1]

Peter's answer set the standard for how the earliest Christians initiated new converts: "Repent, and let every one of you be baptized in the name of Jesus Christ for the remission of sins; and you shall receive the gift of the Holy Spirit."[2] This same pattern is found throughout the New Testament for both Jews and non-Jews who converted to the Jesus sect.

The biblical concept of repentance first requires a reasoned understanding of God's standards of good and evil. This understanding then provokes feelings of regret for living in rebellion against those standards. A person is then motivated to turn away from self-determination and from actions contrary to God's will. These contrary thoughts and actions are called sin. In turning away from self-determination, a person turns to God, beginning a new life.[3]

For converts to the Jesus sect, water baptism symbolized the washing away of sins. Peter declared that baptism is to be in the name of Jesus Christ, tying repentance to the acceptance of Jesus as the Messiah and of his sacrificial death as the substitute that pays the penalty for sin. Peter taught that the believer would then receive the Holy Spirit.

Repentance and water baptism are inseparably linked together in the book of Acts. The baptism ceremony was carried out in two parts. Converts were first immersed in water for the forgiveness of sin.[4] Then the apostles laid hands upon the initiates, symbolizing the immersion of the Holy Spirit. (Later this ritual would be carried out by church elders.)

In Acts 8 a deacon named Philip traveled to Samaria, where he "preached the things concerning the kingdom of God and the name of Jesus Christ [and] both men and women were baptized."[5] When the apostles in Jerusalem heard of these baptisms they sent Peter and John to teach the new converts. They arrived in Samaria but found that the Holy Spirit had not come upon any of those baptized because "They had only been baptized in the name of the

Lord Jesus." The apostles "laid hands on them and they received the Holy Spirit."[6]

The concept that human beings could interact with the Spirit of God was not new to the early Christians. In the Old Testament the Spirit of *Yahweh* was primarily the source of spiritual perception, wisdom and special abilities [7] even physical strength.[8] God's Spirit inspired prophets with visions and divine messages. King David, in a prayer of repentance, implored, "Do not cast me away from Your presence, do not take your Holy Spirit from me."[9] The manifestation of the Holy Spirit was no less than the presence of God.

The prophets told of a time when God would restore the descendants of Abraham to the Promised Land and would put his Spirit in them.[10] This hope of a future pouring out of God's Spirit was a major promise of what the prophets called the New Covenant.[11] The early Christians declared that this time of the pouring out of God's Spirit had begun with the events of Pentecost less than two months after the crucifixion of Jesus.

Christian Initiation

When God instituted a covenant with Abraham he gave him a "sign" of the covenant—on the eighth day after birth, all male children were to be circumcised. This initiated Israelite males as participants in the covenant and marked them as God's special people.[12] To refuse circumcision was to willfully remove one's family from God's covenant.

As Gentiles converted to the Jesus sect, the issue of circumcision became a major point of contention. The question that had to be answered was, "Is physical circumcision an initiation rite required for Gentiles who choose to participate in the New Covenant?"

This debate would rage for decades. It was the primary reason for the first church conference in 49 AD and a major issue in many of Paul's writings. The conclusion of the apostles was that baptism, followed by the receiving of the Holy Spirit, was to be the required initiation rite for the followers of Jesus as the Messiah. This rite applied to both Jew and Gentile.

The apostles found the rationale for this change in the covenant initiation ritual in Old Testament passages. When the Israelites stood on the threshold of the Promised Land God told them of a time when "the LORD your God will circumcise your heart and the heart of your descendants, to love the LORD your God with all your heart and with all your soul..."[13]

In his letter to the Colossians, the apostle Paul merged the Old Testament ideal of circumcision of the heart with water baptism and receiving of the Holy Spirit. He wrote, "In Him [Christ] you were also circumcised with the circumcision made without hands, by putting off the body of the sins of the flesh, by the circumcision of Christ, buried with Him in baptism, in which you were also raised with Him through faith in the working of God, who raised Him from the dead."[14]

For Paul, the person who accepted Jesus as the Messiah wasn't merely professing a faith in his sacrificial substitution. Instead, through immersion, the convert was symbolically participating in Christ's death and resurrection, emerging out of the water into a new life guided by God's Spirit.[15]

The Jesus Sect Expands Beyond Jerusalem

Jesus' followers formed a community in Jerusalem, sharing their possessions and worshipping at the Jewish temple. Jews and proselytes from all over the Roman Empire had seen or heard about the remarkable events of Pentecost when "tongues of fire" appeared on Jesus' followers. Some of these travelers joined the new Jewish sect.

At first the Sanhedrin tried to stifle this radical movement by arresting the leaders. The more the Jewish authorities tried to stamp out the sect, the more their ranks swelled. Even priests began to respond to the message that Jesus was the prophesied Messiah.[16]

Laying on of Hands

The purpose of "laying on of hands" in the Bible is to set apart a person, persons or things for a special blessing, office, duty or purpose of God.

Genesis 48:13-16	Confirming a birthright.
Leviticus 8:1-36	Setting aside the tabernacle and priests for God's service.
Numbers 8:5-11	Setting aside the tribe of Levi for service to God.
Numbers 8:12; Leviticus 1-7	Setting aside sacrifices for the worship of God.
Numbers 27:18-23; Deuteronomy 34:9	Commissioning or ordaining into an office.
1 Samuel 16:13; Matthew 19:13-15; Mark 10:13-16; Luke 18:15-17	Blessing children.
Acts 8:9, 12-13, 14-20; Acts 19:1-7	Receiving the Holy Spirit.
Acts 6:1-8; 13:1-3	Ordaining deacons and elders in the church.
Acts 9:17-18; 28:8; James 5:14	Healing the sick.

The first internal struggle of the Jesus sect involved a controversy between the "Hebrews," or Jews from Judea and the surrounding area, and "Hellenists," or Jews with some background in the Greek world. (Some have suggested that the differences were based on language, culture or geographic origins). The Hebrew group was accused of taking care of their widows but ignoring their Hellenist sisters. The apostles solved the problem by setting aside six Hellenist Jews and one proselyte to this task.[17]

Stephen, one of the men selected to serve the Hellenist widows, was confronted by men from the Synagogue of the Freedmen in Jerusalem. This synagogue was comprised of freed slaves or descendants of freed slaves from far-flung corners of the Roman Empire. Men of the synagogue conspired to spread lies about Stephen. Confronted by an angry crowd, Stephen chastised them for rejecting Jesus as the Messiah. They stoned him to death and the Jesus sect had its first martyr.[18]

The Apostle Peter was among the first to respond to a request from a Gentile God-fearer to be baptized. While resting on a roof top terrace, Peter saw a vision of a sheet filled with animals forbidden as food in the *Torah*. He also heard a voice say "kill and eat" and "what God has cleansed you must not call common."

Soon afterwards, he was called to the house of a Roman centurion named Cornelius. Peter told Cornelius that by Jewish law, in this case oral tradition, he was forbidden to enter the house of a Gentile, but God had showed him in a vision not to call any man "common or unclean." Cornelius and his household were then baptized.[19] The explicit and profound meaning of the vision, explained by Peter, concerned the equal relationship between Jews and Gentiles in the new Messianic community.

A challenge now facing the Jesus sect was determining how to obey Christ's command to spread the gospel beyond the confines of Judea to the rest of the world. The sect would find a receptive audience in the synagogues of the *Diaspora*.

The Synagogue

The Jewish population of the Mediterranean area in the first century is estimated to be as high as five to six million. Synagogues existed from Alexandria to Ephesus and from Babylon to Rome itself. Here a Jew could find a little piece of Jerusalem wherever he traveled throughout the Roman Empire.[20]

The synagogue insured that the Jews, scattered far from Israel, maintained their distinct culture and religion. Unable to take part in the temple sacrifices and rituals, *Diaspora* Jews turned to the synagogue to participate in communal prayer and worship. Martin Goodman, in *Rome and Jerusalem*, comments: "The synagogue as an institution for mass moral education was indeed unique in the Roman world, not least because the closest parallels, the philosophical schools, generally confined their clientele to the intellectual elite. For the Jews in the land of the diaspora, the local synagogue was the main place to which they went for religious edification. It was not a holy place, and worship in the form of sacrifices (as in the Jerusalem Temple) could not be performed there, but it did provide an opportunity for communal prayer and, above all, for teaching."[21]

Because there were so many synagogues, there were more opportunities for non-Jews to be attracted to the God of Israel. Proselytes were Gentiles who converted to Judaism by worshipping the Jewish God, living by his moral code, undergoing circumcision and experiencing a ritual washing. Philo wrote that proselytes were given the same grace from God as Jews and were to be respected in Jewish society.[22] In practice, these converts were probably welcomed into the synagogues with varying degrees of acceptance and suspicion.

Other Gentiles, known as "God-fearers," worshipped the God of Israel but remained uncircumcised. God-fearers observed the Sabbath and moral teachings of Judaism, and avoided idolatry. Because they refused circumcision, God-fearers were not accepted as full participants in ritual worship, but were accepted at Sabbath and holy day observances.[23]

(Circumcision was a tremendous obstacle, not only because of the physical pain, but because of the cultural difference. Greeks idealized the human body, seeing any cuttings or tattoos as destruction of beauty. Circumcision would have been viewed as marring the perfect form.)

Josephus mentioned these Gentile converts, calling them "those that worshipped God." He wrote, "And let no one wonder that there was so much wealth in our temple, since all the Jews throughout the habitable earth, and those that worshipped God, nay, even those of Asia and Europe, sent their contributions to it, and this from very ancient times."[24]

Gentile converts to Judaism were common enough for the Roman Tacitus to notice and write, "Proselytes to Jewry adopt the same practices [avoiding intermarriage and accepting circumcision], and the very first lesson they learn is to despise the gods, shed all feelings of patriotism, and consider parents, children and brothers as readily expendable."[25]

Philo's Description of the Synagogue

"...for it was invariably the custom, as is desirable on other days also, but especially on the seventh day, as I have already explained, to discuss matters of philosophy; the ruler of the people beginning the explanation, and teaching the multitude what they ought to do and to say, and the populace listening so as to improve in virtue, and being made better both in their moral character and in their conduct through life; in accordance with which custom, even to this day, the Jews hold philosophical discussions on the seventh day, disputing about their national philosophy, and devoting that day to the knowledge and consideration of the subjects of natural philosophy; as for their houses of prayer in the different cities, what are they, but schools of wisdom, and courage, and temperance, and justice, and piety, and holiness, and every virtue, by which human and divine things are appreciated, and placed upon a proper footing?"[26]

The participation of Gentiles in Judaism wasn't a new concept. From the time of the Exodus there had been those who wished to join Israel and worship its God.

The Alien Resident

The *Torah*, or Law, detailed the relationship between the native-born Israelite and the "stranger" or "sojourner" who accepted *Yahweh*, joining Israel as a resident alien. The *Torah* lists many instructions about how to treat resident aliens. Deuteronomy 10:17-19 states, "For the LORD your God is God of gods, and Lord of lords, the great God, mighty and awesome, who shows no partiality nor takes a bribe. He administers justice for the fatherless and the widow, and loves the stranger, giving him food and clothing. Therefore love the stranger, for you were strangers in the land of Egypt."

In the *Torah*, the resident aliens received both equal punishment and equal rights under the law. The Ten Commandments contain instructions to include sojourners in the Sabbath rest.[27] A resident alien could even bring offerings to the tabernacle.[28] A sojourner who blasphemed God or committed murder was subject to the same death penalty as a native son.[29]

The Hebrew Scriptures contain the beautiful love story of Ruth, a Moabite, who joined Israel to remain with her mother-in-law. Her choice meant worshipping Israel's God, and eventually marrying an Israelite named Boaz. Boaz and Ruth are listed by Matthew in the lineage of Jesus.[30] In Israel's later history the prophet Isaiah declared blessings on the "sons of the foreigner who join themselves to the LORD, to serve Him, and to love the name of the LORD, to be His servants—everyone who keeps from defiling the Sabbath, and hold fast My covenant...."[31]

By the first century, the scattered synagogues of the *Diaspora* included a substantial number of non-Jews who followed the tradition of joining themselves to the God of Israel.

Antioch, Syria

Outside of Judea, the earliest followers of Jesus were Jews, proselytes and God-fearers drawn from the synagogues of the *Diaspora*. Because of this, the Jesus sect was primarily an urban movement. The followers of Jesus were first called "Christians" at Antioch, Syria.[32] The ruins of ancient cities give us glimpses into marvelous villas, temples, public buildings and engineering feats such as aqueducts, but there was another side to the cities where the first Christians congregated.

In Antioch the streets were narrow and most people lived in small apartments stacked on top of each other. The population of Antioch around the end of the first century is estimated at 150,000. Given the physical size of the city, the crush of people was staggering. Sociologist Rodney Stark in *The Rise of Christianity* notes that "the population density of Antioch was roughly 75,000 inhabitants per square mile or 117 per acre. As a comparison, in Chicago today there are 21 inhabitants per acre; San Francisco has 23, and New York overall has 37. Even Manhattan Island has only 100 inhabitants per acre—and keep in mind Manhattanites are spread out vertically, while ancient cities crammed their populations into structures that seldom rose above five stories."[33]

Livestock sharing living space in ground floor tenements made conditions worse, as did sewage systems that couldn't handle the massive amounts of waste. Filth, disease and crime were rampant. Factoring in the high infant mortality rate, life expectancies in many Roman cities was only around 30 years.[34] Like many cities of the time, Antioch's history involved a continual chain of natural disasters, devastating fires, famines, earthquakes, epidemics and wars.[35]

In the cities of the Roman world, we discover a great dichotomy between the squalid conditions of the poor and the wealth of the rich and the middle class, supported by trade and slavery.

The Apostle Paul

It is ironic that the man most responsible for spreading the message of Jesus to the Roman world beyond Judea started out as the Sanhedrin's instrument of Christian persecution.[36]

Saul of Tarsus, called Paul, was truly cosmopolitan with a background in both Pharisaic Judaism and Greek culture. He was born around the first of the century in Tarsus, a city in Asia Minor situated at the northeast corner of the Mediterranean Sea. Tarsus was the capital of the Roman province of Cilicia.[37] At the time of Paul's birth, Tarsus was already an ancient city tracing its origins to a time before Abraham. The city was famous as a seat of learning and philosophy, and for the industries of linen weaving and tent making.[38]

Paul, who attested to a strict Jewish upbringing, was of the tribe of Benjamin. In his younger years, Paul traveled to Jerusalem to be tutored by the famous teacher Gamaliel.[39]

Gamaliel was the grandson of Hillel, the founder of a great school of the *Torah*. Sometimes called Gamaliel the Elder, he was the first in Judaism to be given the title of *rabban*, "our master, our great one," instead of the normal title of *rabbi*, which means "my master." Gamaliel appears in the New Testament as counseling the Sanhedrin to treat Jesus' apostles with caution.[40] One of Gamaliel's well-known sayings is, "Get yourself a teacher, and keep away from doubtful matters, and never tithe by guesswork."[41] His importance in first century Judaism is attested by the Talmudic lament, "When Rabban Gamaliel the Elder died, the glory of the Law ceased and purity and abstinence died."[42]

Paul's success in Judaism is shown by his connection to the Sanhedrin; by his consenting to the stoning of Stephen; by his zeal in persecuting the followers of Jesus; and by his expertise in the "traditions of the fathers."[43]

By trade, Paul was a tentmaker, following a tradition that states, "It is good to follow a workaday occupation as well as to study the

Torah, for between the two one forgets to sin."[44] He was fluent in Aramaic, Greek and Hebrew. His quoting of Hellenistic poets in both public speaking and writings illustrates a fluency in Greek literature.[45]

Paul was a Roman citizen by birth.[46] The Bible doesn't give us a physical description, although his enemies in Corinth made the accusation that "his bodily presence is weak, and his speech contemptible."[47]

The defining event in Paul's life was his encounter with the resurrected Christ, when he first began to realize that many Jews had "stumbled" over Jesus as the prophesied Messiah.[48] Christianity's main persecutor became its prominent defender, leading the effort to spread the message about the Kingdom of God and about Jesus as the Christ throughout the Roman Empire. His greatest success would be among the God-fearers of the synagogues.

Taking the Message to Samaria

When the followers of Jesus launched their mission beyond Judea, they confronted a religious leader in Samaria who "converted" and then claimed to possess a deeper understanding of God and Jesus than the original disciples. The ideology promoted by this new teacher would have profound effects on how Christianity developed during the next three centuries.

8

SIMON, SAMARITANS AND SYNCRETISM

Simon the Sorcerer. Simon the Magician. Simon Magus. His appearance in one biblical passage launched numerous stories concerning his teachings, his influence on early Christianity, and even his death. Was he really worshipped as a god? Who were the Samaritans who gave birth to his sect?

Sometimes it is difficult to separate historic fact from fable. In this case, the truth is stranger than fiction. Before we explore the historic Simon the Sorcerer and his cult, let's first look at the origins of the Samaritans and their place in first century Judaism.

Origins of the Samaritans

After King Solomon's death around 930 BC, Israel divided into two nations. In the south, Rehoboam ruled Judah, while in the north Jeroboam ruled 10 of the tribes, known as Israel. The Northern Kingdom of Israel had its capital in Samaria. Jeroboam was afraid that when the people of Israel traveled to the temple in Jerusalem for the annual pilgrimage festivals, they would reunite with their southern compatriots. His solution was to modify Israel's worship of the God of Abraham, Isaac and Jacob.

Jeroboam negated the need for the northern tribes to travel to Jerusalem by building shrines and erecting idols in Israel. He ordained priests who weren't from the tribe of Levi and established new holy days. Though he introduced idols into the national religion, Jeroboam didn't give up the worship of Israel's God, even entreating the prophet of *Yahweh* when his son became ill. Jeroboam didn't deny the existence of God; he simply created a new way to worship Him.[1]

Israel was ruled by a succession of kings who continued to practice Jeroboam's syncretized religion. Eventually, in 722 BC, the Assyrians invaded the Northern Kingdom. Most of the inhabitants were taken into slavery and scattered throughout the Assyrian Empire. The Assyrians then imported other peoples into the land of Israel, also known as Samaria after the name of the capital.

Local Deities

Most ancient religions did not disavow the gods and goddesses of other cultures, but believed in the power of local deities. It was common for pagans to accept that the God of Israel possessed great power in the land of Israel, but had little sway outside his own locality.[2] During time of Israel's king Ahab, the Syrians were wary of fighting in the hills because the Israelite "gods are gods of the hills. Therefore they are stronger than we; but if we fight against them in the plain, then surely we will be stronger than they."[3]

The peoples the Assyrians imported into Samaria soon wanted to placate the God of Israel. 2 Kings 17:24-26 states: "Then the king of Assyria brought people from Babylon, Cuthah, Ava, Hamath, and from Sepharvaim, and placed them in the cities of Samaria instead of the children of Israel; and they took possession of Samaria and dwelt in their cities. And it was so, at the beginning of their dwelling there, that they did not fear the LORD; therefore the LORD sent lions among them, which killed some of them."

"So they spoke to the king of Assyria, saying, 'The nations whom you have removed and placed in the cities of Samaria do not know the rituals of the God of the land; therefore He has sent lions among them, and indeed they are killing them because they do not know the rituals of the God of the land.'"

An Israelite priest of Jeroboam's syncretized religion was sent to teach the Samarian immigrants how to worship the God of Israel. These people simply accepted Israel's God as the local deity and worshipped him along with the gods from their homelands.[4] 2 Kings 17:33 concludes, "They feared the LORD, yet served their own gods—according to the rituals of the nations from among whom they were carried away."

Judah eventually followed their northern brothers into captivity, but at the hands of the Babylonians. While the Jews were under the Babylonian thumb the Persians conquered Babylon.

In the 500s BC the Jews began returning from their exile. The Persians allowed a Jew named Zerubbabel, who served in the royal court, to begin to rebuild Jerusalem. The Samaritans opposed the rebuilding project. They sent a letter to the king of Persia in an attempt to sabotage Zerubbabel's leadership.[5] The temple was eventually built and the Samaritans lived as an ethnic and religious minority in the land of the Jews.

Josephus records numerous confrontations between Jews and Samaritans, "for such is the disposition of the Samaritans...that when the Jews are in adversity they deny that they are kin to them, and then they confess the truth; but when they perceive that some good fortune hath befallen them, then immediately pretend to have communion with them, saying that they belong to them, and derive their genealogy from the posterity of Joseph, Ephraim and Manasseh."[6]

Jesus and the Samaritans

At the time of Jesus, the Samaritans still occupied an area between Galilee in the north and Judea in the south. A Roman may have considered the Samaritans just another Jewish sect, but mainstream Judaism rejected them as pretenders and interlopers.

This animosity is illustrated by an incident that occurred when Jesus passed through the region. The local Samaritans shunned Jesus, and his disciples responded by asking permission to call fire from heaven to destroy the Samaritan village. [7]

In this environment, imagine the chagrin of Jewish religious leaders over Jesus' use of a Samaritan as a hero in what is commonly called the parable of "The Good Samaritan." Jesus interacted with Samaritans and performed healings among them. He also commanded his disciples to teach in Samaria after his resurrection.[8]

In another incident, Jesus was traveling in Samaria and asked a woman for a drink. She answered, "How is it that you being a Jew, ask a drink from me a Samaritan?" John adds, "For Jews have no dealing with Samaritans."

Jesus continued to talk with her until she concluded that he was a prophet and confronted him with, "Our fathers worshipped on this mountain [Mount Gerizim], and you Jews say that in Jerusalem is the place where one ought to worship."

Jesus answered by explaining that a time is coming when "true worshippers will worship the Father in spirit and truth...." The Samaritan woman showed some knowledge of the Hebrew Scriptures when she replied, "I know that the Messiah is coming.... When He comes, He will teach us all things."[9]

The woman told others of this conversation and many Samaritans were drawn to Jesus and responded to his teachings. Though the acceptance of Jesus as the Messiah became common in Samaria, this doesn't mean they abandoned the religious syncretism of their ancestors. It was from this outcast community that the followers of Jesus came into contact with Simon the Sorcerer.

Simon the Sorcerer

A deacon named Philip preached the gospel in Samaria in the late 30s AD. Many Samaritans, including Simon the Sorcerer, were baptized. Luke gives a number of important details:

- When Simon came into contact with the Christian church, he was already the leader of a syncretized Samaritan religion using demonic powers.

- Simon was baptized by Philip.

- He tried to buy the Holy Spirit and office of apostle. This is the origin of the term "simony" for the purchase of religious offices.

- Peter recognized Simon's false conversion. Simon's response was to ask Peter to act as intercessor between him and God.[10]

Peter confronted the leader of the Samaritans and rejected him from the Jesus sect. Simon disappears from the biblical account after Peter's rebuke. Substantial details about Simon's life do not appear until the second century. Justin Martyr wrote that Simon left Samaria for Rome, where he established his cult and was worshipped as a god.[11]

From Justin Martyr, and other second and third century writers, it is possible to piece together some of the teachings of the Simonians as they continued to expand after Simon's death. The ninth edition of the *Encyclopedia Britannica* summarizes these sources, creating a picture of their teachings:

"Simon, it would appear, declared himself to be 'the highest power"—the Supreme God Himself; he taught that among the Jews he manifested himself as the Son, in Samaria as the Father, and among other nations as the Holy Spirit. Helena, whom he had purchased in a brothel in Tyre, he considered to be the mother of all, by whom he had called all the angels and archangels into being. She had proceeded from him, had been initiated into his purposes, had voluntarily come down from heaven and became the mother of the angels and powers who created this world; but after the completion of her work she had been laid under bonds by her own children, the world creating angels, who desired to be independent, and who knew not the first father Simon; they imprisoned her in a human body, and subjected her to every affront; she had to migrate out of one body into another..."[12]

The Simonians espoused a peculiar interpretation of history and the Bible. They concluded that many of the famous Helens of history, including the Helen of Homer's Iliad, were reincarnations of the original Helena. Simon finally rescued her from her body-to-body migration, thus fulfilling Jesus' parable of the lost sheep. Simon was worshipped as "The Lord" and Helena as "The Lady." Simonians believed that Simon appeared in many forms in order to bring salvation to lost humanity.

They taught that matter, being a product of lesser beings instead of the supreme god, was evil. Man possessed a "divine spark" that could be released from the physical world to a better life in the spirit world. Since matter was inherently evil, Jesus' appearance as the Jewish Messiah was a vision. This dualism between matter and spirit, darkness and light, good and evil, was foundational to Gnosticism, a religious system that would become a major threat to Christianity. The Simonians would develop into one of the first Gnostic sects. Gnosticism promoted a radical dualism between the body, which was material and therefore evil, and the soul, which could be released from the bondage of the body through the mystery of *gnosis*, or knowledge.

According to the Simonians, angels originally created the universe. These angels were then put in charge of governing the world but failed because of rivalries among themselves. Old Testament prophets and laws were inspired by these world-creating angels. Simon, who claimed to be a manifestation of the supreme god, came to free humankind from the harsh laws imposed by the lesser, creator angels. The result of this lawlessness was that "Believers in Simon were at liberty to do what they will, for by the grace of Simon should men be blessed—but not on account of good works."[13]

This myth would appear in various forms among other Gnostic sects. *The Aprocrython of John*, written in the second century, tells of a light-being named Sophia, who decided to create a god without permission from the supreme god. The result was a being who, with the aid of angels, created the world and humanity.[14]

Catholic bishop Eusebius wrote around 325 AD, "Simon, we are given to understand, was the prime author of every heresy.... Their more secret rites, which they claim will so amaze a man when he first hears them that, in their official jargon, he will be wonderstruck, are indeed something to wonder at, brim-full of frenzy and lunacy, and of such a kind that not only can they not be put down in writing; they involve such appalling degradation, such unspeakable conduct, that no decent man would let mention of them pass his lips. For whatever could be imagined more disgusting than the foulest crime known has been outstripped by the utterly revolting heresy of these men, who make sport of wretched women, burdened indeed with vices of every kind."[15]

Nearly three hundred years after Peter confronted Simon, Eusebius lamented that the Simonians still existed: "It is an astonishing fact that this is still the practice of those who to the present day belong to his disgusting sect. Following in their progenitor's footsteps they slip into the church like a pestilential and scabby disease, and do the utmost damage to all whom they succeed in smearing with the horrible, deadly poison concealed on them. By now, however, most of them have been expelled-just as Simon himself, when his real character had been exposed by Peter, paid the appropriate penalty."[16]

The Simonian Cult

How could the leader of an insignificant Samaritan religion influence the development of a syncretized Gnostic cult that battled Christian groups for centuries? Their success is rooted in the age in which the cult existed.

The Roman world of the first century was a dynamic scene of religious and philosophical debate. The interaction of ideas and freedom of religion was cultivated by the internal roads, culture and relative safety of the empire. Luke captured the spirit of the age when he wrote of the Apostle Paul's speaking to the Areopagus, "For all the Athenians and the foreigners who were there spent their time in nothing else but either to tell or to hear some new thing."[17] The Simonians found fertile ground in this age of syncretism.

Judaism hadn't escaped this dynamic exchange of philosophies and ideas and by the time of Jesus it was fragmented into different sects. Christianity experienced explosive growth in the decades following the death and resurrection of Jesus. The fledgling Christian church soon found itself in a struggle with paganism and Gnosticism. Paul's letters to Galatia, Corinth and Colossae reveal congregations already struggling with ideas that would develop into gnostic doctrines.

Death of Simon

The Simonians were participants in a religious amalgamation sweeping the Roman Empire in the first four centuries AD. These early Gnostics absorbed various doctrines and ideas from Judaism, paganism, Christianity and Greek philosophy, and introduced their teachings to other Gnostic sects.

It's difficult to sort fact from fiction in the life of Simon the Sorcerer. Even his death is shrouded in myth. One story claimed that in order to prove his divinity he was buried alive so he could be resurrected in three days and nights. According to the account, he's still there today.[18] The Acts of Peter, written toward the end of the second century, claimed that Simon deceived many by flying around like a giant bird until Peter called upon God and Simon fell to the ground and broke his leg. Following an operation he died.[19]

There is no doubt that Simon's Hellenistic-Gnostic cult was influential in Samaria and Rome. Traces of his cult's teachings still flourish today in segments of Christianity, which traces its origins as much to the religious amalgamation of the first four centuries AD as to the teachings of Jesus Christ.[20]

9

TURNING THE WORLD UPSIDE DOWN

Saul was a changed man. The fearsome persecutor of Jesus' disciples entered the synagogue of Damascus and confessed to the dumbfounded congregants that Jesus was the prophesied Messiah. Jesus' followers were leery about fellowshipping with their former antagonist. When he arrived in Jerusalem, he was shunned by the congregation. A popular disciple named Barnabas vouched for Saul and began to mentor the former persecutor. Saul became a spokesman for Jesus, arguing with the Hellenistic Jews in Jerusalem.[1]

Barnabas and Saul ended up in Syrian Antioch, where the congregation commissioned them to spread the gospel. Saul, who became known to history by his Greek name Paul, traveled the eastern Mediterranean preaching "the word of God in the synagogues of the Jews."[2]

In Pisidian Antioch Paul elegantly reasoned from the Scriptures that Jesus of Nazareth was the prophesied Messiah.

Here Paul introduced a major theme that would be at the center of his teachings: "Therefore let it be known to you, brethren, that through this Man [Jesus] is preached to you the forgiveness of sins; and by Him everyone who believes is justified from all things which could not be justified by the Law of Moses."[3]

Many Jews and proselytes believed his message and the next Sabbath almost the entire city came to hear Barnabas and Paul speak. Because of the large numbers of Gentiles who responded, some of the Jews became jealous, turning against the two missionaries and expelling them.[4]

When Paul and his entourage traveled to Iconium the situation turned violent. Luke recorded in Acts 14:1: "...they went together to the synagogue of the Jews, and so a great multitude both of the Jews and of the Greeks believed." The Greeks who met every Sabbath in the Jewish synagogue were obviously proselytes and God fearers. These God-fearers spread Barnabas' and Paul's message to pagans throughout the city. The people became so divided over what they heard that antagonists plotted to kill the two preachers and they were forced to flee.[5]

Paul continued his pattern of introducing his message in the synagogues of the cities where he visited. His greatest successes seemed to be among the Gentile proselytes and God-fearers. These first Christians, both Jews and Gentiles, didn't view Paul's teachings as a new religion, but as an extension of Judaism. Their religion had the same God, the same Scriptures and the same ethical code. This was true even when Christian groups separated from the Jewish synagogue.

W.H.C. Frend points out in *The Rise of Christianity*: "Once a Christian community had been established, Paul's letter to its members presupposed a synagogue background. He used the normal Jewish salutations to them. The content breathed the Septuagint and synagogue society. The Corinthians were reminded, for instance, 'that our fathers were all under the cloud' (1 Cor. 10:1)—what would that have meant to a pagan?"[6]

Paul expected his readers to have a comprehensive understanding of the Hebrew Scriptures. To grasp Paul's points concerning the Old and New Covenants in his Epistle to the Galatians, a reader would have to possess a detailed knowledge of the Genesis account concerning Abraham and Sarah.[7] In 1 Corinthians 9:8-9 Paul quoted Deuteronomy 25:4 to teach congregational support of the ministry and in 1 Corinthians 14:34 he used the "law" as instructions for the role of women in church services. In his Epistle to the Romans Paul not only quoted Moses but he also cited extensively from 1 Kings, Psalms, Proverbs, Isaiah and Hosea.[8]

A pagan convert to Christianity, without an extensive background in the Hebrew Scriptures, would have difficulty understanding Paul's teachings. On the other hand, Paul's writings would make sense to proselytes and God-fearers because of their association with Judaism. God-fearers and proselytes would become the link between Christianity and the pagan world.

The Jerusalem Conference

While God-fearers and Jewish proselytes were already schooled in the Scriptures, a question the followers of Jesus faced was how were pagan converts to be initiated into the covenant people? Were pagans required first to become full-fledged Jewish proselytes through circumcision? Were they to adhere to all the ceremonies of the *Torah*, and even the oral law, before becoming Christians?

A group of Christians, who were also Pharisees, began to teach the new converts, "Unless you are circumcised according to the custom of Moses, you cannot be saved."[9] Barnabas and Paul were incensed that these kinds of stipulations were being forced on Gentiles who were just coming to the knowledge of God and Christ.

A conference was called in Jerusalem with the apostles and elders to settle this heated controversy. After intense debate Peter told the assembled church leaders, "Men and brethren, you know that a good while ago God chose among us, that by my mouth the Gentiles should hear the word of the gospel and believe. So God, who knows the heart, acknowledged them by giving them the Holy Spirit, just as He did us, and made no distinction between us and them, purifying their hearts by faith. Now therefore, why do you test God by putting a yoke on the neck of the disciples which neither our fathers nor we were able to bear? But we believe that through the grace of the Lord Jesus Christ we shall be saved in the same manner as they."[10]

Barnabas and Paul explained how God had blessed their work in spreading the gospel to the Gentiles. James, the brother of Jesus, gave the final speech. He showed how the calling of Gentiles to God was a fulfillment of prophecy by quoting Amos 9:11-12: "After this I will return and will rebuild the tabernacle of David, which has fallen down; I will rebuild its ruins, and I will set it up. So that the rest of mankind may seek the LORD, even all the Gentiles who are called by my name, says the LORD who does all these things."

James announced his conclusion, "Therefore I judge that we should not trouble those from among the Gentiles who are turning to God, but that we write to them to abstain from things polluted by idols, from sexual immorality, from things strangled, and from blood. For Moses has had throughout many generations those who preach him in every city, being read in the synagogues every Sabbath."[11]

This decision was a watershed event in Christian history. The church would not be limited to Judea by being tied to the temple, practicing circumcision and in many ways indiscernible from other Jewish sects except for their belief in Jesus as the Messiah. The apostles believed that they had a commission to bring all people into the worship of Israel's God and to the knowledge of Jesus Christ.

Scholars still debate the effects of this transition on primitive Christianity as well as the significance for us today. Many commentators believe the result of the Jerusalem Conference was freedom for Gentiles from all the laws of the *Torah*. This interpretation sees the four regulations declared by James as issues enforced only for the sake of Jewish conscience. The council's decision laid the foundation for the future development of a new Gentile Christianity based in a Hellenistic instead of Jewish model.

Another common view is that in his proclamation, James was referencing seven commandments God gave to humanity through Noah before there was a distinction between Israelite and Gentile. The rabbis taught that these seven commandments were: to practice justice; to abstain from blasphemy; to refrain from idolatry; to avoid bloodshed: to forgo robbery: and to quit eating flesh torn from a wild animal.[12]

Do either of these interpretations really explain the decision of the Jerusalem Conference? This seminal passage needs to be evaluated carefully. Some points to consider are:

- Peter affirmed that Gentiles and Jews were involved in the same process of salvation.

  Peter stated, "But we believe that through the grace of the Lord Jesus Christ we shall be saved in the same manner as they." The apostles didn't believe that there were two means of salvation, one for Jews through the Law of Moses, and one for Gentiles through faith in Jesus Christ. Both were being saved by God's grace exhibited in Christ.

  A few years earlier, Peter argued before the Jerusalem leaders that uncircumcised God-fearers, such as the Roman centurion Cornelius, who had come to accept Jesus as the Messiah, were to be accepted as equal members of the Jesus sect. He now supported Barnabas' and Paul's argument that pagan converts didn't need circumcision (and the Pharisaical requirements of becoming Jewish proselytes) to become equal disciples of Jesus.

  It is important to remember that the issues of the Jerusalem Conference were initiated by Pharisee Christians. Peter said that Pharisaical legalism was a "yoke" that even the Jews couldn't bear.[13]

- James didn't want to overwhelm the new converts as they were "turning to God."

The four regulations aren't the all-inclusive elements of Christian conduct, but are the beginning steps of conversion for those coming out of paganism.

Even a casual reading of the New Testament shows that Gentile converts were expected to do more than these four regulations in order to be considered Christians. Paul's writings contain numerous lists of behaviors that disqualify a person as a Christian. In Galatians he wrote, "Now the works of the flesh are evident, which are: adultery, fornication, uncleanness, lewdness, idolatry, sorcery, hatred, contentions, jealousies, outbursts of wrath, selfish ambitions, dissensions, heresies, envy, murders, drunkenness, revelries, and the like; of which I tell you beforehand, just as I told you in past time, that those who practice such things will not inherit the kingdom of God."[14]

To the Corinthians he penned, "Do you not know that the unrighteous will not inherit the kingdom of God? Do not be deceived. Neither fornicators, nor idolaters, nor adulterers, nor homosexuals, nor sodomites, nor thieves, nor revilers, nor extortioners, will inherit the kingdom of God. And such were some of you. But you were washed..."[15]

It is also true that the codes of Christian behavior contained in the New Testament are much more extensive than the seven Noahic commandments taught by the rabbis. These four regulations defined by the Jerusalem Conference are a minimal starting point for people with no background in Judaism. They are not an end-all explanation of Christian moral behavior or relationship with the *Torah*.

- If the only reason for the four regulations was not to offend Jews, then there was no moral reason for continuing them over time.

It is absurd to conclude that Jesus' apostles decided that the only reason for forbidding fornication was to make Gentile Christians socially acceptable to Jewish Christians. (As one teenager said after hearing a minister expound this explanation, "So let me get this straight, I can do it with her as long as she isn't Jewish?") If social discourse is the only reason, then we'd have to ask why it was acceptable for Jewish Christians to socialize with Gentile Christians who were drunkards, habitual liars, thieves, or blasphemers. All of these sins were offensive to Jewish Christians.

- The *Torah* was still being taught every week in the synagogue.

At this stage the early Christians were not yet fully separated from the synagogue. Hebrew Scriptures were still holy for the followers of Jesus. These Scriptures could be found only in the Jewish synagogues, where new converts to Christianity could attend with Jewish proselytes and God-fearers.

The Jerusalem Conference determined that pagans didn't have to become Jewish proselytes before becoming Christians. The apostles established that circumcision was not a requirement for salvation. (This teaching was already accepted by many Jews and God-fearers in the *Diaspora* and affirmed by the Jerusalem church leaders years earlier by their acceptance of Cornelius.) The apostles also established a starting point for pagans by stating four required regulations. What the Jerusalem Conference did not conclude was that the entire moral code of the Hebrew Scriptures was annulled for those turning from paganism to God.

This was not the last time Paul would face the Pharisaical circumcision party. For the Pharisees who converted to

Christianity, their customs died hard and this issue would be debated for decades.

It is important to recognize that this issue wasn't a simple divide between Jewish Christians and Gentile Christians. After all, it was the Jewish elders and apostles in Jerusalem who decreed that Gentile converts didn't have to submit to the requirements of the Pharisee Christians. It was also common for *Diaspora* Jews to observe the Sabbath with uncircumcised God-fearers as fellow followers of God.

Turning the World Upside Down

After the Jerusalem Conference Paul returned to Antioch in Syria, but became restless to revisit the areas where he and Barnabas had founded churches.[16] On this journey he continued the same pattern of meeting with Jews and God-fearers on the Sabbath.

One instance, recorded in Acts, illustrates Paul's continued success among God-fearers: "And on the Sabbath day we went out of the city to the river, where prayer was customarily made; and we sat down and spoke to the women who met there. Now a certain woman named Lydia heard us. She was a seller of purple from the city of Thyatira, who worshipped God. The Lord opened her heart to heed the things spoken by Paul." Paul baptized Lydia's entire household.[17]

When Paul came to the synagogue of Thessalonica "as his custom was, [he] went in to them, and for three Sabbaths reasoned with them from the Scriptures." A "great multitude of devout Greeks, and not a few of the leading women," responded to Paul's teaching that Jesus was the Christ. As in other cities, some Jews were envious of his success. They accused Paul and his companions, saying they had "turned the world upside down..."[18]

In the synagogue of Berea many Jews believed Paul's message, but also "not a few of the Greeks, prominent women as well as men." The Bereans were known for their daily diligence in searching the Hebrew Scriptures to "find out whether these things were so."[19]

A notable thread in the successes of the earliest Christians is that not only were Jews, God-fearers and some pagans attracted to Paul's message, but many women were among his converts. These women played an important role in the formation of the first Christian communities.

Paul Goes to Athens

The city of Athens visited by Paul was still a philosophical center of the Roman world. Among its many temples and altars to a plethora of gods and goddesses, Athens even bore the mark of Rome with a temple to Augustus.

It was common for Paul to see statues of pagan deities in the many cities he visited, but the sheer magnitude of Athenian idolatry grieved him. He "reasoned in the synagogue with the Jews and Gentile worshippers and in the marketplace daily with those who happened to be there."

His message was centered on the person of Jesus and the resurrection of the dead. He came to the attention of some Stoic and Epicurean philosophers who invited him to enter into a debate before the Areopagus. There Paul began his speech: "Men of Athens, I perceive that in all things you are very religious; for as I was passing through and considering the objects of your worship, I even found an altar with this inscription: TO THE UNKNOWN GOD."

He used this inscription on a pagan altar to launch into a description of God as the Creator. God was "Lord of heaven and earth" who transcended any human attempts to worship him with temples and idols. Paul expounded the common origins of all human beings and claimed that the Creator God is the designer of history. In spite of God's unfathomable greatness, human beings can have a personal relationship with him.[20]

Paul then did something remarkable for a man schooled in Pharisaical Judaism. Instead of quoting from Hebrew Scriptures, which would have been rejected by both Epicureans and Stoics, he made his point by quoting from a pagan poet named Epimenides.

According to the Roman biographer Plutarch, hundreds of years before Paul's arrival, a Cretan writer named Epimenides was known for more than his verse. He was "possessed of knowledge in all the supernatural and ritual parts of religion." Epimenides was called to Athens to drive out a mysterious plague involving "strange appearances."[21] Paul quoted from a poem written by the pagan Epimenides about Zeus to reveal the Unknown God to his pagan audience.

He concluded by declaring that the Creator God is going to judge the world through the Anointed Man whom he has raised from the dead. The idea of the resurrection of the dead turned some of the philosophers against Paul, while others said they would like to hear him speak on another occasion. Some who heard believed Paul's message.[22]

Paul's education in Tarsus became a tool for reaching pagans with the gospel. He could launch his discussion in religious and cultural terms they understood, but it must be remembered that his purpose was never to syncretize Christianity with paganism.

Paul left congregations in many of the cities he visited. One congregation, in the heart of Greece, would present a new battle for the beleaguered apostle. In addition to keeping the Pharisaical Christian party at bay, Paul would have to deal with the intrusion of Hellenism. The congregation was in the city of Corinth.

Did the Early Church Worship on Sunday?

Acts records that the followers of the Apostle Paul continued to worship on the Sabbath, so when did Christians begin to worship on Sunday to honor the resurrection of Jesus? It is commonly believed that a passage in Acts 20 shows that some Christians had changed from Sabbath to Sunday worship by the mid 50s.

Acts 20:7 states, "Now on the first day of the week, when the disciples came together to break bread, Paul, ready to depart the next day, spoke to them and continued his message until midnight."

First, notice that the passage doesn't mention a worship service, but a gathering to eat a meal. It is also important to understand that in both the Old and New Testaments, days started at sunset, not midnight as reckoned in the 21st century.[23] In the following verses Luke described how a man fell asleep in the middle of the night, tumbling off a balcony to his death. The apostle miraculously raised him up, but did not finally leave until daybreak.[24]

Since days were reckoned to start at sunset; since Acts 20:7 is describing a gathering that took place on the first day of the week; and since the meeting started late in the evening, then the time of the meeting must be what we call Saturday night.[25] If these events took place after sunset on Sunday night, then this would have been the second day of the week.

This passage about Christians gathering to eat a meal Saturday night and then listening to Paul does not prove that Christians in the 50s were meeting on Sunday mornings to honor the resurrection of Jesus.

The book of Acts records the story of Paul's journey throughout the *Diaspora*, preaching the gospel to Jews and God-fearers in the synagogues on the Sabbath. Even after pagans began to convert, Paul gave no instructions to observe Sunday as a day of worship.

10

THE WISDOM
OF THE WORLD

The Greek city of Corinth was perfectly situated as a place of two seaports. It sat on a peninsula allowing merchants to service ships from gulfs to the east and west of the city center. When Roman legions sacked Corinth in 146 BC, they left it partially ruined and sparsely populated. Julius Caesar rebuilt the city as a Roman colony in 44 BC.

By the time Paul arrived in Corinth in the early 50s AD, it was again a thriving metropolis. Like most ancient seaports, Corinth was known for its multiculturalism, lucrative business opportunities, religious diversity and seamy pleasures. Its name spawned a Greek verb meaning "to practice fornication."[1]

After his arrival, Paul met two fellow Jews. Aquila and his wife Priscilla had been expelled from Rome during the reign of Claudius. They worked together with Paul making tents during the weekdays, while Paul "reasoned in the synagogue every Sabbath, and persuaded both Jews and Greeks." The apostle experienced such good success among the Corinthians that even the leader of the synagogue believed the gospel. Paul stayed in Corinth for a year and a half.[2]

After leaving Corinth, Paul wrote numerous letters to the church he left behind. Two of these letters are included in the New Testament, yielding insight into a congregation not only dealing with Jewish issues such as circumcision, but also with a syncretism of Hellenistic paganism with Christianity that threatened to change the nature of the gospel.

1 Corinthians

In 1 Corinthians, Paul wrote to a congregation torn by strife and divisions. Some people followed a charismatic teacher named Apollos. Some professed loyalty to Paul or Peter. Others asserted that they didn't follow any man, but declared allegiance to Christ alone. 1 Corinthians contains some of the harshest correction Paul poured out on any congregation. He corrected them for factions, chided them for tolerating sexual immorality, and offered marital advice. Members were reprimanded for taking each other to the secular courts. Paul also explained how individuals preaching the gospel were worthy of financial support. He even chastised some members for visiting prostitutes and others for participating in pagan feasts. The list of offenses Paul wrote against included drunkenness during the Passover communion, conflicts over church authority and the role of women in the congregational meetings. Amid all this confusion, the Corinthians were proud of their spiritual knowledge and gifts, especially the gift of tongues.

Early in the letter Paul revealed two sources of the Corinthian problem: "For Jews require a sign, and Greeks seek after wisdom...."[3] Paul then reminded the congregants that they hadn't been called by God because they were intellectuals or important people in society, but because God had deliberately called the weak and unimportant to reveal his great power.[4]

In 1 Corinthians 2:6 Paul denounced the "wisdom of the age." In Athens, he publicly argued the worthlessness of idolatry and

Greek philosophy compared to the truth about the Creator God. Writing to the Corinthian church, he condemned the "wisdom" of the Hellenistic age, especially as Hellenistic thinking rejected Jesus as the crucified Jewish Messiah. He went on to write, "Let no one deceive himself, if anyone among you seems to be wise in this age, let him become a fool that he may become wise."[5] The wisdom of God was a mystery to those schooled in Hellenistic wisdom. It could not be discovered by human reason alone, but only through the power of God's Spirit working in a person's mind.[6]

Here Paul took his attack on paganism a step further than he had in Athens. To the Athenian philosophers, Paul had declared the Creator God who transcends idols and temples of stone. To the Corinthian Christians he denounced idolatry as demon worship. He told those with one foot in Christianity and the other in paganism, "You cannot drink the cup of the Lord and the cup of demons; you cannot partake of the Lord's table and the table of demons."[7]

It is obvious that Paul was writing to an audience well schooled in the Old Testament. In 1 Corinthians Paul quoted from Exodus, Deuteronomy, Job, Psalms, Isaiah and Jeremiah. He quoted from Genesis to command men to stop cavorting with prostitutes; he condemned idolatry by recounting a story from the time when the Israelites wandered in the wilderness; and he testified that the proof of Jesus as the Christ is found in the Hebrew Scriptures.[8]

One of the most fascinating statements in this letter concerns the Corinthians' observance of the Passover season. He tells them, "Your glorying is not good. Do you not know that a little leaven leavens the whole lump? Therefore, purge out the old leaven, that you may be a new lump, since you are truly unleavened. For indeed Christ, our Passover, was sacrificed for us."

The meaning of this passage can be understood only in the context of the Jewish observance of the Passover and Days of Unleavened Bread. The Passover lamb was slain and leavening was removed from the home in remembrance of the exodus. Paul taught that the substitute sacrifice of the Passover lamb was a symbol for the substitute sacrifice of Jesus Christ. For Christians, leavening now took on a unique symbolism as the invasive quality of sin in the mind of the sinner.

He continued, "Therefore, let us keep the feast, not with old leaven, nor with the leaven of malice and wickedness, but with the unleavened bread of sincerity and truth."[9] Even at this stage in the 50s, the church was observing the Passover festival.

The issue of circumcision doesn't seem to have been a major problem in Corinth. Paul briefly mentions it: "Circumcision is nothing and uncircumcision is nothing, but keeping the commandments of God is what matters."[10] Notice that Paul believed the *Torah* to be modified in relationship to Gentile circumcision, but he still expected both Jewish and Gentile Christians to continue to obey its moral instructions, such as the Ten Commandments, and to observe festivals, such as the Passover.

The Resurrection

A difficult concept for some Corinthians was the resurrection of the dead. Paul had faced the same problem with the Athenian philosophers. Because of the Hellenistic belief in the immortal soul, these Greeks struggled with the idea of the resurrection of the dead.

Paul's premise in 1 Corinthians concerning the resurrection is based entirely on the reality of the death and resurrection of Jesus Christ. If Christ didn't rise, then all people are lost in their sins and condemned to eternal punishment. Paul argued that followers of Jesus who have died are "asleep;" and if there is no resurrection, then they have no hope of future life. Christ is the "first fruits" of a future harvest of followers who will be raised from the dead.[11]

The Hellenistic idea was that at death a person's soul would be freed from the material body. It would then go to *Hades*, or in some scenarios, return to the realm of the heavenly bodies where it would exist as a ghostly spirit. When considering the idea of the resurrection, the logical question for them was, "What kind of body do resurrected people possess?"

Paul answered with, "There is one glory of the sun, another glory of the moon, and another glory of the stars; for one star differs from another star in glory. So also is the resurrection of the dead. The body is sown in corruption, and raised in incorruption. It is sown in dishonor, it is raised in glory. It is sown in weakness, it is raised in power. It is sown a natural body, it is raised a spiritual body. And there is a spiritual body."[12]

This resurrection was to happen at the return of Jesus Christ when all saints would be changed in a "twinkling of an eye." Paul declared to the Corinthians, "For this corruptible must put on incorruption, and this mortal must put on immortality."[13] In his letter to the Corinthians, Paul echoed the Old Testament teaching concerning death as "sleep." He proclaimed the promise of a future resurrection in connection with the coming of the Messiah.

The Spirit of the Law
In his ministry, Paul related to Jews in the context of their Jewish culture. As he put it: "to those who are under the law, as under the law, that I may win those who are under the law...." He related to Gentiles as those who were "not under the law" so that they, too, could come to God. This didn't mean that he thought that God's law didn't apply to Gentiles. He wrote that in relating to Gentiles he was not "...without law toward God, but under the law toward Christ."[14]

In 2 Corinthians 3 the apostle further explains what it means to be under Christ's administration of the law. Paul proclaimed that the Corinthians were his letter of commendation because in them the Spirit of God had written God's message, not on "tables of stone," but on "tables that are of hearts of flesh."[15]

The "tables of stone" is an obvious reference to the Ten Commandments given to Moses by God. The "hearts of flesh" is referring to Old Testament passages such as Jeremiah 31:31-36, in which the prophet told of a time when God would make a New Covenant with the people of Israel. In this passage God said, "I will put My law in their minds, and write it on their hearts...."

The prophet Ezekiel also wrote of a time when God promised, "Then I will give them one heart, and I will put a new spirit within them, and take away the stony heart out of their flesh, and give them a heart of flesh, that they may walk in My statutes and keep My judgments and do them; and they shall be My people and I will be their God."[16]

It was prophecies like these that Jesus' apostles declared were beginning to be fulfilled by the pouring out of the Holy Spirit on Pentecost 50 days after his resurrection. Paul expanded this interpretation by stating that the New Covenant instituted a change in the relationship of the individual to the law, "for the letter kills, but the Spirit gives life."[17]

The Ten Commandments written on tables of stone are glorious because they spring from the mind of God, but they can only condemn those who disobey. When a person turns to God by accepting Jesus as the Christ, then the "ministry of the Spirit" writes those same laws on that person's heart and mind. The Ten Commandments are no longer external rules, but an internal force guided by God's Spirit.

Paul reminded his audience that when Moses carried the Ten Commandments down from Mount Sinai, his face shone from being in the presence of God. Because of the brightness, Moses covered his face with a veil.[18] Paul claimed that a metaphorical veil remained on the hearts of Jews who hadn't accepted Jesus as the Messiah. Because of that veil they weren't able to understand the "reading of the Old Testament." He concluded that it is the Lord Jesus who defined righteousness and it is his image that Christians are to reflect in their thinking and actions.[19]

Paul supplied the Corinthian church with a template for relating to the *Torah*. The Ten Commandments on tables of stone is an external set of rules that demands obedience against the will of the natural man. God, through the ministry of the Spirit, writes his law on the hearts of men, producing loving, faithful obedience to its righteous requirements. The ministry of law on stones was glorious because it reveals the mind of God. The ministry of the Spirit has greater glory because it introduces the mind of God into human beings.

Paul and Hellenism in Corinth

What can we establish from the book of Acts and Paul's writings to the Corinthians as his response to Hellenistic society? We can draw some important conclusions about Paul's teachings to both Jewish and Gentile Christians from these sources.

- The Jewish God is the only God; any form of idolatry is unacceptable for Christians.

- Jesus is the prophesied Jewish Messiah sent for all humanity. Only through faith in him as the Christ can a person be justified before God.

- The Old Testament law hadn't been abrogated, but Christians had been given a new relationship with the law through a new relationship with the Lawgiver. The Ten Commandments are no longer enforced from tables of stone, but are written in the character of those who turn to Christ through the ministry of the Spirit. Christians are expected to obey these commandments, not only in the letter, but in the Spirit. Paul's teachings echo Jesus' teachings in the Sermon on the Mount.

- Christians should believe in the resurrection of the dead, as taught in the Hebrew Scriptures.

- Jesus is returning to establish God's Kingdom on the earth.

Paul pioneered the movement to ensure that the Christian church didn't become a Pharisaical sect of Judaism. In his mission to the Corinthians, he also led the battle against the Hellenizing of Christianity. This battle would intensify throughout the next century, until Primitive Christianity began to fade into the shadows, replaced by a new Hellenized orthodoxy.

In the 60s, just when Paul's work was at its zenith, the early Christians would face annihilation.

11

A DERANGED EMPEROR AND THE DESTRUCTION OF THE JEWISH TEMPLE

Christianity experienced substantial growth during its first three decades. People who had seen Jesus now spread his message to Jewish communities throughout the Roman Empire. Non-Jews began to find the teachings about a personal God attractive. There was scattered persecution, but many congregations experienced relative peace. The Jerusalem church, led by Jesus' original apostles, served as a central point to resolve doctrinal disputes.

No one was more responsible for the spread of Christianity in these early decades than Paul of Tarsus. Paul wasn't one of Jesus' original disciples. In fact, he had vehemently persecuted Christians. After his conversion to Jesus' teachings, Paul spread his message beyond Judea. Christian communities sprang up in Cyprus, Asia Minor and Greece—even in Rome itself.

In a six-year period, between 64 and 70, two events profoundly affected the early Christian church. The first event happened in

Rome; the second in Jerusalem, where Rome exerted its power against the ancient city of David.

Nero

There had been trouble between Romans and Jews during the reign of Claudius. Many Jews were exiled from Rome in 49, and some of those expelled were of a Jewish sect called "Christians."[1]

Claudius was replaced by his nephew Nero in 54. Two writers supply fascinating insight into the strange world of Emperor Nero.[2] Suetonius (c. 69-140), an imperial secretary under Emperor Hadrian, had access to many official documents. These documents supplied the groundwork for his book, *The Lives of the Twelve Caesars*. The Roman historian Tacitus (c. 55-117) also recorded many details of life in the Roman Empire.

Nero was born around 37 AD. When he was three, his father died and Nero was subsequently adopted by his uncle Claudius. He was tutored by Seneca, one of the great intellectuals of his day. By the time Nero was 11, he was fond of performing in plays and craved public acclaim. His mother Agrippina convinced Claudius to name her son his successor. When Claudius did, she had the emperor poisoned. Nero ascended to the throne at age 17 and soon rejected Seneca's guidance.

The egotistical emperor fancied himself a great singer, painter, actor and intellectual; he promoted plays and public games; and he showed interest in science and architecture. Exhibiting little interest in extending the empire, Nero instead worked to create a distinct Roman culture.

Displaying excessive worry about reviews and awards, Nero changed the rules of the Olympics so that music was declared a sport. He went so far as to pass a law making it illegal to leave the theater when he was performing. One time he condemned a pregnant woman to death for going into labor while he was singing. On occasions, men "died" during his performances, only to miraculously revive once they were carried from the theater.

He would flatter judges and bribe contestants during competitions. Once during a chariot race, he became so weary he couldn't finish but was still declared the victor. The judges were handsomely rewarded.

One of Nero's favorite pastimes was to disguise himself, go out into the streets late at night, and assault drunks returning from the taverns. He also liked to break into shops and steal anything he could carry. After he was almost beaten to death by a man who caught him with his wife, the emperor learned to travel on these forays with armed guards.

Nero was bisexual. He committed incest with his mother, had sex with boys and committed adultery with any woman who caught his eye. He alienated some of the priests when he broke the law by taking a Vestal Virgin. (Vestal Virgins were a group of six virgin priestesses who served in the temple of the goddess Vesta.) He once made a man a eunuch, dressed him in a wedding gown, and married him in a public ceremony. During one spectacle, prisoners were stripped naked and tied to stakes while the emperor, dressed as a wild animal, attacked the captives.

This infamous emperor squandered a vast fortune in riotous living. One of his extravagant houses had a number of rooms, each a mile long. An enormous bathtub from his palace is on display in the Vatican museum.

Nero eventually decided to murder his mother, but the task proved to be quite an undertaking. He failed three times to poison her; he built a bed with a collapsing canopy to crush her in her sleep, but she was warned; and he designed a ship for her that fell apart and sank. To his surprise, Agrippina managed to swim to shore. Finally, he had her stabbed to death.

Rome's Great Fire

Rome suffered a devastating fire in 64, destroying 10 of the 14 precincts. Although no one really knows how the fires started, some Romans blamed Nero.

Tacitus supplies this account: "Terrified, shrieking women, helpless old and young, people intent on their own safety, people unselfishly supporting invalids or waiting for them, fugitives and lingerers alike—all heightened the confusion. When people looked back, menacing flames sprang up before them or outflanked them. When they escaped to a neighboring quarter, the fire followed—even districts believed remote proved to be involved. Finally, with no idea of where or what to flee, they crowded unto the country roads, or lay in the fields. Some who had lost everything—even the food for the day—could have escaped, but preferred to die. So did others, who had failed to rescue their loved ones. Nobody dared to fight the flames. Attempts to do so were met by menacing gangs. Torches, too, were openly thrown in, by men crying out that they acted under orders. Perhaps they had received orders. Or they may just have wanted to plunder unhampered."[3]

Rumors spread that Nero had failed to stop the fire, or had instigated it, so he could rebuild parts of the city, which had decayed into dilapidated tenements. He needed someone to blame. The Christians, disliked by pagans and Jews, fit the mold, especially since it was believed Christians taught that the world was going to be destroyed by fire.

Tacitus continues: "Nero fabricated scapegoats—and punished with every refinement the notoriously depraved Christians (as they were popularly called). Their originator, Christ, had been executed in Tiberius' reign by the governor of Judea, Pontius Pilatus. But in spite of this temporary setback the deadly superstition had broken out afresh, not only in Judea (where the mischief had started) but even in Rome. All degraded and shameful practices collect and flourish in the capital."[4]

In the Roman Circus, Christians were crucified or dressed in animal skins and torn apart by wild dogs. Nero used other Christians as human torches to light nighttime parties. Even some hardened Romans began to pity them, "For it was felt that they were being sacrificed to one man's brutality rather than to the national interest."[5] Suetonius states: "The Christians, men given to a new and wicked superstition, were put to death with grievous torments."[6]

Tradition states that Christian leaders Peter and Paul were both killed in 68, the same year the army and Senate overthrew Nero. When capture was imminent, Nero committed suicide with the help of an aide. Periodic persecutions of Christians would continue throughout the empire for hundreds of years.

Nero Fiddled while Rome Burned

Historian Cassius Dio (c. 155-230) wrote a vivid account of the burning of Rome years after the event. "While the whole population was in this state of mind and many, crazed by the disaster, were leaping into the very flames, Nero ascended to the roof of the palace, from which there was the best general view of the greater part of the conflagration, and assuming the lyre-players garb, he sang the 'Capture of Troy,' as he styled the song himself, though to the eyes of the spectators it was the Capture of Rome."[7] In accounts like this we find the origins of the phrase: "Nero fiddled while Rome burned."

The Christian View of the End of the World

The Roman accusation that a conflagration was part of the Christian view of God's judgment on humanity was rooted in fact. In the Gospels, Jesus' unique teaching concerning hell is illustrated by his use of the word *Gehenna*.

Gehenna was the name of a ravine south of Jerusalem, known in English as the Valley of Hinnom. In Judah's earlier history the *Valley of Hinnom* was the sight of a cult involving child sacrifice. Kings Ahaz and Manasseh both participated in this pagan cult, which was eventually destroyed by King Josiah.[8] *Gehenna* became associated with God's judgment when the prophet Jeremiah proclaimed that God would punish Judah for this unspeakable horror and turn the Valley of Hinnom into the "Valley of Slaughter."[9]

During the days of Jesus, the Valley of Hinnom was an ever-burning garbage dump, a smoldering depository for Jerusalem's refuse and dead animals.[10] On numerous occasions, Jesus used *Gehenna* as symbol for God's judgment on the wicked.

Jesus painted a graphic word picture when he used this smoking, stinking trash heap as an object lesson of God's punishment on those who are evil when he said, "If your right eye causes you to sin, pluck it out and cast it from you; for it is more profitable for you that one of your members perish, than for your whole body to be cast into hell *(Gehenna)*."[11] Jesus taught that both body and soul are destroyed in *Gehenna*.[12]

A few years after Rome suffered its great fire, the Apostle Peter wrote of a time when the earth will be consumed by fire: "But the day of the Lord will come as a thief in the night, in which the heavens and the earth will pass away with a great noise, and the elements will melt with fervent heat; both the earth and the works that are in it will be burned up."[13]

Gehenna was synonymous with the term "lake of fire" used in the writings of John. Towards the end of the century, the Apostle John wrote of a time when both "Death and Hades were cast into the lake of fire."[14] After this event, God will create a "new heaven and a new earth...."[15]

Jerusalem's Destruction

In 66 AD the Jews rebelled against Roman occupation. By the spring of 70, Roman troops surrounded Jerusalem. Hundreds of thousands of pilgrims, there to celebrate Jewish holy days, swelled the city's population. Under the strangling grip of the Roman siege, famine swept through the city.

Josephus interviewed eyewitnesses and described the misery as "unspeakable." Friends and family members fought each other for scraps of food. People waylaid the dying, hoping to find a morsel. "Moreover, their hunger was so intolerable, that it obliged them to chew everything, while they gathered such things as the most sordid animals would not touch, and endured to eat them; nor did they at length abstain from girdles and shoes; and the very leather which belonged to their shields they pulled off and gnawed: the very wisps of old hay became food to some...."[16] In the end, Jerusalem was sacked and the temple burned. Josephus estimated that more than 1,100,000 Jews were killed in the war and 97,000 were taken prisoner.[17]

The Jerusalem Church Survives the Siege

Because Jesus had lived in Nazareth, the Christians in Jerusalem became known as Nazarenes.[18] Eusebius (c. 263-339) records that the Jerusalem Church, because of a revelation from God, survived the city's destruction by fleeing to a town called Pella.[19]

In the fourth century, Bishop Epiphanius wrote of a Jewish-Christian sect, still existing in Pella and other places, who were the direct descendants of the early Jerusalem church. They used an Aramaic version of Matthew, observed the seventh-day Sabbath, kept the clean and unclean meat laws of Leviticus, taught circumcision, believed in the resurrection and proclaimed the divinity of Jesus as the Son of God.[20]

After the deaths of most of Jesus' original apostles and the loss of the Jerusalem church's prominence, Christian congregations experienced a leadership vacuum. In this vacuum, individual congregations developed diverse practices and doctrines.

The New High Priest

Written shortly before the destruction of the Jewish temple, The Epistle to the Hebrews explained for Christians their relationship to the Jewish priesthood and sacrificial system. The letter opens with an extended argument, using the Old Testament as evidence, proving that Jesus is not an angelic being, but the unique Son of

Josephus and Tacitus
Write of Miraculous Signs

Josephus wrote that survivors of the siege of Jerusalem told stories of miraculous signs. Christian writers later claimed that these signs inspired the Jerusalem church to flee the city.

According to Josephus, a comet blazed across the night sky for an entire year. Another star, which appeared as a sword, stood over the city. A heifer being led by priests to be sacrificed dropped a lamb. One day the massive eastern temple gate, which took 20 men to shut, opened by itself. Supernatural chariots and soldiers were seen massing in the clouds. "Moreover, at that feast which we call Pentecost, as the priests were going by night into the inner [court of the temple,] as their custom was, to perform their sacred ministrations, they said that, in the first place, they felt a quaking, and heard a great noise, and after that they heard a sound as of a great multitude, saying, 'Let us remove hence.'"[21]

The Roman historian Tacitus echoes Josephus' account. He told of ghostly armies fighting in the sky above Jerusalem and of a light shining on the temple while a supernatural voice called out that the gods were departing. Tacitus claimed that the Jews were inspired to continue fighting because of prophecies foretelling rulers from Judea who would set up a universal empire. His imperial pride led him to conclude that these prophecies actually predicted the reigns of Vespasian and Titus.[22]

God who is "appointed heir of all things, through whom He made the worlds."[23] The author wrote that Jesus came in the flesh to conquer the devil and that upon his resurrection he became the High Priest serving God in the heavenly temple.[24]

Christ's priesthood replaced the need for the Levitical priesthood. Tithes were to be given to Christ instead of the Levites,

"For the priesthood being changed, of necessity there is also a change in the law."[(25)] Hebrews confirms that Christ's priesthood is eternal and superior in all ways to any human priesthood. The value of Christ's universal sacrifice negated the need for daily animal sacrifices.[(26)]

Moses had been instructed to create the original tabernacle modeled after a pattern shown to him while on Mount Sinai. The utensils of the physical tabernacle were "copies" of the spiritual reality of the throne of God.

Hebrews explains that the Old Covenant was flawed because the Israelites were flawed. They could not fulfill their part of the covenant because the Holy Spirit did not dwell within them. The author of Hebrews quotes from the prophet Jeremiah to support his teachings that Christ is the High Priest of a New Covenant in which God will "put My laws in their minds and write them on their hearts...."[(27)]

The letter states that the foundational doctrines of those who approached God through Jesus as the divine High Priest are "repentance from dead works and of faith towards God, of the doctrine of baptisms, of laying on of hands, of resurrections of the dead, and of eternal judgment."[(28)]

Hebrews shows the way for a Christian theology without the need for the Jewish temple, sacrificial system or priesthood. After the destruction of the Jewish temple, the followers of Jesus would proclaim that salvation would be available to all as they look to a High Priest who had offered himself as a sacrifice for all people and serves in the heavenly temple of God.

The Church Survives

In spite of persecution and dispersion the Christian movement survived and continued to attract new converts from among Jews, God-fearers and increasing numbers of pagans. What was it about this movement that attracted people even in times of persecution?

12

WHY BECOME A CHRISTIAN?

In the second half of the first century the old pagan gods were losing some of their luster. The public ceremonies, with priests as participants and worshippers as onlookers, were too impersonal. Emperor worship might promote political unity, but it offered little personal comfort. The empire spread multiculturalism, but it also increased discontent with institutionalized religion. Many pagans were looking for a more personal relationship with the gods. Mystery religions were growing in popularity.

The concept of one creator god, as put forth by both Platonism and Stoicism, offered an intellectual answer to spiritual longing. However, the ambiguity of the Platonic or Stoic god supplied little meaning for the common folk. Because of the sheer diversity of religious cults and temples, gods and goddesses were everywhere and people looked for spiritual connections in dreams, astrology, oracles and omens.

A History of Private Life: From Pagan Rome to Byzantium
describes the changes happening towards the end of the first
century: "...the new paganism ceased to be institutionalized. It was
much more informal than the old paganism. Each person could
shape religion as he pleased. In the past, when someone wished
to know the will of the gods, he sought out a priest or oracle: a
legitimate institution. Now, the orders of the gods were conveyed
to individuals in all sorts of ways outside official channels. They
came in dreams, in ominous incidents, in vague presentiments.... In
addition, a whole literature of popular piety made its appearance.
Some of these books were best-sellers that helped to modernize
and 'spiritualize' popular religious practices."[1]

Which leads to an important question: Why would a pagan
convert to a religion rooted in a belief in one God and a Jewish
Messiah? Some answers are found by exploring a few of the major
differences between paganism and early Christianity.

- The Christian belief that God loves humanity.[2]

   For most pagans, life seemed controlled by the irrational
   whims of the gods, expressed in nature's unpredictable
   actions and mysterious omens. The Christian God
   expressed his love for humanity in the sacrificial death of
   his Son Jesus as the substitute for the penalty hanging over
   every person due to rebellion against him and his teachings.

   Pagans could see there was ample proof that Jesus had lived
   and died in Jerusalem. Thousands of people claimed that
   they had seen him after his resurrection. These witnesses
   were so convicted of Jesus' resurrection that they suffered
   martyrdom to defend it. They proposed a new reality—the
   divine Son of God had come in the flesh and now acted
   as High Priest and intercessor between God and humanity.
   This dedication convinced others of the reality of the Jewish
   God as humanity's God.

- The Christian belief in the brotherhood of believers.

Early Christians proposed radical social change. Each person, slave or free, rich or poor, man or woman, had equal value as a child of the Creator. In Christian congregations people from all economic and social strata not only worshipped together, but also formed a brotherhood. Paul proclaimed this brotherhood to the Galatians: "For you are all sons of God through faith in Christ Jesus. For as many of you as were baptized into Christ have put on Christ. There is neither Jew nor Greek, there is neither slave nor free, there is neither male nor female, for you are all one in Christ Jesus. And if you are Christ's, then you're Abraham's seed, and heirs according to the promise."[3]

An example of this new social order is found in Paul's Epistle to Philemon, written around 60 AD. Philemon was a member of the church in Colossae. His slave, Onesimus, had run away to visit Paul, who was under house arrest in Rome.[4]

A History of Private Life: From Pagan Rome to Byzantium explains the complex role of slavery in Roman life: "The Romans lived in unspoken fear of their slaves. Though by nature an inferior being, the slave was a member of his master's family, one whom the master 'loved' and punished paternally and from whom he expected 'love' and obedience in return."[5]

Slaves weren't seen as inferior because of race or tribe, but because they were members of a lower social class. Slaves were considered to be intellectual and emotional children and were often addressed as "little ones" or "boy." Marriages between slaves had no legal status, and families could be separated and sold at the master's whim. Punishment could be cruel, even deadly.[6]

Seneca promoted a more "humane" treatment of slaves when he wrote: "It is creditable to a man to keep within reasonable bounds in his treatment of his slaves. Even in the case of a human chattel one ought to consider, not how much one can torture him with impunity, but how far such treatment is permitted by natural goodness and justice, which prompts us to act kindly towards even prisoners of war and slaves bought for a price (how much more towards freeborn, respectable gentlemen?), and not to treat them with scornful brutality as human chattels, but as persons somewhat below ourselves in station, who have been placed under our protection rather as assigned to us as servants. Slaves are allowed to run and take sanctuary at the statue of a god; though the law allows a slave to be ill-treated to any extent, there are nevertheless some things which the common laws of life forbid us to do to a human being."[7]

The Stoic philosopher chided a well-known Roman for feeding the blood of slaves to his lampreys to fatten them. He attempted to motivate slave owners to better treatment by stating, "Cruel masters are pointed at with disgust in all parts of the city, and are hated and loathed."[8]

Paul admonished slaves to be obedient to their masters and to look to God for their reward. He encouraged masters to treat slaves with kindness and fairness, reminding the masters of God's judgment as Master of both slaver owner and slave.[9]

In his Epistle to Philemon Paul attacked the concept of the inferiority of slaves. The letter began with Paul showing appreciation for Philemon's "love and faith which you have toward the Lord Jesus and toward all the saints." Paul implored Philemon, "I appeal to you for my son Onesimus, whom I have begotten in my chains, who was unprofitable to you, but now is profitable to you and to me. I am sending him back." (Paul used the term "begotten" to describe Onesimus as a convert, or an individual who had been baptized and had received the Holy Spirit.)

Paul said that he would like Onesimus to stay and assist him in his ministry, but didn't want to do so without Philemon's permission. He then wrote, "For perhaps he departed for a while for this purpose, that you might receive him forever, no longer as a slave but more than a slave—a beloved brother...." Paul implores Philemon to receive Onesimus "as you would receive me. But if he has wronged you or owes anything, put that on my account."[10]

The apostle, who declared that God through Christ had torn down barriers between Jew and Gentle, stripped the underpinnings from Roman slavery by promoting a brotherhood of believers.

- The Christian promise of salvation and the resurrection of the dead.

Roman belief in the afterlife was as complex as the varied religions flourishing throughout the empire. Many Romans approached what happened after death with a sense of ambiguity. Others denied any existence beyond this life.[11]

The official Roman religion adapted the Greek concept of the underworld. The Greek god of the underworld, named *Hades*, became the Roman god *Pluto*. The place of the dead was also called *Hades*. This land of the dead was divided into different regions. The ghostly souls of the virtuous existed in beautiful, carefree surroundings; the souls of the common man existed as wandering shadows; and the souls of the wicked endured various states of torture.

Others accepted the Platonic concept that human souls originated in heaven and could return to heaven. Titus, as his army prepared to attack Jerusalem, attempted to rouse his legionnaires by reminding them that while the souls of those who die from disease or old age may decay into oblivion, the souls of those who die in battle ascend to take their places among the stars.[12] The belief that the stars and planets were souls inspired an obsession with astrology.

The Christian teaching was a radical insight into the afterlife. Paul taught that Christians were "seeking immortality."[13] The early church followed the teaching of the Hebrew Scriptures that upon death a person entered a state of "sleep," but would experience a future bodily resurrection. Christians proclaimed that at Christ's return his followers would be resurrected with "spiritual bodies."[14]

- The Christian hope in the face of life's difficulties.

The Christian God was understood to be the God of history and prophecy. He has a purpose for humanity. His nature is consistent in both love and justice. Christian meaning is found in God's loving interaction with his children in the present world, and Christian hope is in the Kingdom of God, which will be established at Christ's Second Coming. At that time, Christ will overthrow human tyranny, bringing peace and prosperity to all nations. The difficulties in this life prepare the Christian for the coming glorious life of the resurrection.

- The Christian belief that evil can be explained by the influence of Satan, who is the present "god of this world."[15]

Paul tells Christians in Ephesus: "And you He made alive, who were dead in trespasses and sins, in which you once walked according to the course of this world, according to the prince of the power of the air, the spirit who now works in the sons of disobedience, among whom also we all once conducted ourselves in the lusts of our flesh, fulfilling the desires of the flesh and of the mind, and were by nature children of wrath, just as the others."[16]

In the same letter he encourages his audience to, "Put on the whole armor of God, that you may be able to stand against the wiles of the devil. For we do not wrestle against flesh and blood, but against principalities, against powers, against the rulers of the darkness of this age, against spiritual hosts of wickedness in heavenly places."[17]

For Christians, the daily personal struggles are part of a greater battle between good and evil. Present human governments are ruled by evil, invisible beings, but those beings can't thwart God's plan of salvation. Faithful, dedicated members of the church are assured victory by God's work through Christ as Savior, High Priest and Messianic King.

- The Christian promotion of a strong ethical code rooted in ancient Scriptures.

Both Jews and non-Jews of the first century who accepted the biblical God and Jesus as the Messiah became the "elect." The elect were to live by a code of morality rooted in the precepts of the *Torah* as interpreted by Jesus and his apostles. The indwelling of God's Spirit made it possible for true believers to live by the spirit of the law instead of the letter. Old Covenant instructions concerning circumcision, ceremonies and sacrifices were then defined as physical examples of the spiritual work of Christ.

Christianity in Transition

While the influences of Christianity would be felt throughout a wide area, adherents of the new religion would in turn be influenced by the social customs and former religious practices of new converts. Each Christian community planted outside of Judea had a unique local culture and religious background. Paul's letters to Rome, to the Greek cities of Corinth, Philippi and Thessalonica, and to the Asian cities of Galatia, Ephesus

Edward Gibbon

For centuries the definitive study of the Roman Empire has been the expansive *The Decline and Fall of the Roman Empire* by Edward Gibbon (1737-1794). Gibbon concluded that Christianity spread beyond the confines of Judea because: "I. The inflexible, and, if we may use the expression, the intolerant zeal of the Christians, derived, it is true from the Jewish religion, but purified from the narrow and unsocial spirit which, instead of inviting, had deterred the Gentiles from embracing the Law of Moses. II. The doctrine of a future life, improved by every additional circumstance which could give weight and efficacy to that important truth. III. The miraculous powers ascribed to the primitive church. IV. The union and discipline of the Christian republic, which formed an independent and increasing state in the heart of the Roman empire."[18]

and Colossae, are all written to congregations with serious issues concerning doctrine, practice and morality. These letters speak of local schisms; sectarian Jewish Christians requiring Gentiles to be circumcised; pagan practices being accepted as Christian observances; the introduction of proto-Gnostic customs, such as angel worship and asceticism; and some believers viewing God's grace as a license for immorality.

New leaders opposed the apostles by promoting themselves as teachers of a better Christianity. They introduced radical ideas, including the belief that Jesus was an apparition who didn't have an actual physical body. Others taught that the Ten Commandments had been abrogated, or brought in Hellenized pagan concepts that harkened to the time of Simon Magus.

Paul warned the elders of the Ephesian church, "For I know this, after my departure savage wolves will come in among you, not sparing the flock. Also, from among yourselves men will rise up, speaking perverse things, to draw away disciples after themselves."[19]

The Apostle Peter, writing in the 60s, told the churches at large, "...there will be false teachers among you, who will secretly bring in destructive heresies, even denying the Lord who bought them, and bring on themselves swift destruction. And many will follow their destructive ways, because of whom the way of truth will be blasphemed."[20]

Writing late in the first century, the Apostle John admonished Christians not to believe every spirit but to "test the spirits, whether they are of God." He reminds the Church not to trust every person who claims to bring a message from God.[21]

The diversity of Christian congregations in the late first century is illustrated in John's Revelation, written to seven churches in Asia Minor. This letter shows that the church Paul founded decades earlier in Ephesus had withstood false teachers, but had lost their "first love." The church in Smyrna, while suffering poverty and persecution, remained loyal to the original Christian teachings. The congregations in the cities of Pergamos and Thyatira suffered from heresies and immorality. Sardis was a "dead" church. Philadelphia was praised for being a faithful church, while Laodicea contained a congregation that was condemned as "lukewarm." To the churches in Ephesus and Pergamos John wrote of the dangers of a heretical sect called the Nicolaitans, who were known for sexual immorality and idolatry.[22]

As a new century dawned, Christianity was a minority religion gaining a foothold throughout the Roman Empire, increasingly separated from Judaism, and far from unified in doctrines or practices.

13

PERSECUTION, FORGERIES AND GNOSTICS

The religious movement tracing its origins to Jesus of Nazareth entered the second century in a state of flux. Without the guidance of the original apostles, local groups created distinctive teachings and practices. Non-Jewish converts brought new cultural—and sometimes pagan—influences into the churches. The coming century would witness debates about doctrines and religious observances as well as which books should be included in Scripture and how to understand the nature of Jesus as the Son of God.

Around 100 AD Clement, the overseer bishop of Rome, sent a letter to the Corinthian church chiding them for divisive factions. Clement admonished the congregation with examples of Old Testament personalities, including Cain and Abel, Noah, Jonah, Abraham, and Rahab, as well as the examples of the apostles Peter and Paul. He encouraged the Corinthians to return to a pure faith and to restore leaders of the church whom the congregation had removed. Clement called the Old Testament "sacred Scriptures," showing that at this time the authority of the Hebrew writings were still widely accepted.[1] The following decades would bring heated disputes about the validity of the Hebrew Scriptures for Christians.

A book circulated among many congregations was the *Didache*, or "The Teaching," written between 100 and 120. Some scholars believe it is actually a compilation of earlier writings. In the *Didache* an anonymous author explained that there are two life paths—one that leads to life and another to death. It encouraged unity while instructing Christians to avoid sexual immorality, dishonesty, astrology and abortion.

This small book also contained instructions for various practices, such as baptism and fasting. It addressed the use of bread and wine as Christian religious symbols of Christ's body and blood. Adherents are encouraged to recite Jesus' prayer from the Sermon on the Mount three times daily.[2] They are also instructed to avoid the Jewish practice of fasting on Mondays and Thursdays, and to choose to fast on Wednesdays and Fridays instead.[3]

Letters from Ignatius, a bishop born in Antioch in Syria, provide insight into various Christian communities of the second century. He wrote to churches in Rome and Ephesus, as well as to Polycarp, the bishop of Smyrna. In each case Ignatius admonished Christians to obey their bishops and to reject heresies. Ignatius wrote against those who claimed that Jesus did not come in the flesh, wasn't born of a virgin, and had only appeared to suffer.[4]

The writings of two other men influenced Christian thought in the second century. For one of those writers, his manner of death became attached to his name—Justin Martyr. He completed a number of works between 160 and his death in 165. The other writer was Irenaeus (c. 130-200) of Smyrna. Irenaeus later became the bishop of Lyon in Gaul. In his writings we find a wealth of information about the diversity of Christian groups of the second century.

Persecution

Sporadic Roman persecution of Christians broke out in various regions of the empire. The Romans saw no difference between Christian factions, and they practiced equal opportunity harassment. For some Christians, martyrdom became a divine privilege. Ignatius considered his martyrdom a great honor. In his letter to Rome, he asked Christians not to try to save him from his glorious death.[5]

An interesting account of Christian persecution survives in a letter written around 112 from Pliny the Younger, the Roman governor of Bithynia, to Emperor Trajan. Pliny struggled to determine the exact nature of Christian crimes. He explained to Trajan, "But they declare their guilt or error was simply this— on a fixed day they used to meet before dawn and recite a hymn among themselves to Christ, as though he were a god. So far from binding themselves by oath to commit any crime, they swore to keep from theft, robbery, adultery, breach of faith, and not to deny any trust money deposited with them when called upon to deliver it. This ceremony over, they used to depart and meet again to take food—but it was of no special character, and entirely harmless."

Pliny stated that he tortured two "deaconesses," but found them guilty of no other crime except being Christians. He bemoaned the fact that pagan temples were almost abandoned, but was glad that people were beginning to return to the old ways. Trajan replied that Christians were not to be "hunted out" and that anonymous accusations were not admissible in court.[6]

Jewish Wars with Rome

The Jews once again revolted against the Romans between 115 and 117, this time in North Africa and Egypt. Roman historian Cassius Dio (c. 155-230) painted a bloody and exaggerated picture of the Jewish rebels as barbarians: "Meanwhile the Jews in the region of Cyrene had put a certain Andreas as their head, and were destroying both the Romans and the Greeks. They would eat the flesh of their victims, make belts for themselves of their entrails, anoint themselves with their blood and wear their skins for clothing; many were sawed in two, from the head downwards; others they gave to wild beasts, and still others they forced to fight as gladiators. In all two hundred and twenty thousand persons perished."[7]

The revolt spread to Cyprus, where the death toll was reported at two hundred and fifty thousand. Jews were driven from the island and forbidden to return.[8] Emperor Trajan crushed the revolt in Cyrene and Egypt. In reprisal, he forcibly removed Jews from various parts of the empire.[9]

Around 130 Emperor Hadrian decided to rebuild Jerusalem into a model Roman city populated with non-Jews. Taxes imposed on Jews across the empire were used to support the construction of a number of pagan temples in the new city. In 132 the Jews retaliated. Dio supplies the Roman account of the story: "At Jerusalem he [Hadrian] founded a city in place of the one which had been razed to the ground, naming it Aelia Capitolina, and on the site of the temple of the god he raised a new temple to Jupiter. This brought on a war of no slight importance nor of brief duration, for the Jews deemed it intolerable that foreign races should be settled in their city and foreign religious rites planted there."[10]

In what is called the Bar Kokhba Revolt, the Jews fought a guerilla war, hitting Roman troops and then retreating to underground tunnels and fortifications. Dio states that by 135 the Romans had destroyed 50 "outposts" and "nine hundred and eighty-five of their most famous villages." Jewish deaths from battle, famine and disease were so great that "nearly the whole of Judaea was made desolate." Roman casualties were also very high.[11]

So ended the Jewish nation. In addition, Jews had been nearly exterminated from some segments of the empire. Although they still lived in many cities and villages, they desperately struggled to maintain their distinctive culture and religion. These events would have grave impact on trends growing in Christian congregations.

Forgeries and New Writings

First century Christians accepted the Hebrew Scriptures as the basis for their religious beliefs. The New Testament is filled with hundreds of quotes from the Old Testament proving Jesus was the prophesied Messiah, supporting doctrines and practices of the Primitive Church and explaining right and wrong conduct. The earliest Christians also began to collect new writings they considered inspired by God. The Apostle Peter placed Paul's writings on the same level as Old Testament Scripture.[12]

Scrolls and books were expensive items before the invention of the printing press. Since there were no methods of mass printing, each copy of a work was meticulously reproduced by hand. Congregations wouldn't always have access to all of the Hebrew Scriptures or every book of the New Testament.

In order to become widely read, it was common for a person to write a letter or book and then forge a famous person's signature. This was done either to honor other authors or to cash in on another's name. (Even in his day, Paul warned the church in Thessalonica not to be fooled by forgeries claiming to be written by his hand).[13] In the second and third centuries numerous forgeries, such as the *Gospel of Thomas*, the *Acts of John*, the *Acts of Paul*, and the *Acts of Peter*, were sometimes accepted as authentic scripture by various congregations. These fakes had profound influences on local and regional teachings.

One of the most influential of these early forgeries was the *Epistle of Barnabas*, which appeared around 130. Many Christians considered the letter to be an authentic work of the Barnabas who mentored Paul.[14]

The *Epistle of Barnabas* claimed that the truth given by God to Moses was lost to the Israelites because they worshipped the golden calf before Mount Sinai. The writer stated that the seven-day creation account in Genesis was an allegory of six thousand years of human history followed by a seventh day, or thousand years, when Jesus returns to bring rest to the world. Christians should observe the "eighth day," designated as Sunday, as a special day because it represented the new world to come after the millennial rest.[15]

The epistle taught that when Moses threw down the Ten Commandments in response to Israel's idolatry, God negated their covenant.[16] The Jews were then misled by an evil angel into misinterpreting God's intent for circumcision. The author argued that physical circumcision wasn't the sign of God's covenant with Israel by pointing out that it was common practice among pagan Syrians, Arabs and Egyptians.

This forgery also claimed that the clean and unclean meat laws given in the Old Testament were never intended to be taken literally, but were given as an allegory to teach proper human behavior. The instructions not to eat a pig were intended to teach people not to act like a pig. The command not to eat rabbit was actually a lesson against immorality, "For the rabbit adds an orifice every year; it has as many holes as years it has to live." Instructions were given against eating hyenas because, "this animal changes its nature every year, at one time it is a male, the next time a female."[17] What the author of *Barnabas* lacked in knowledge of animal biology he made up in imagination. His book would have inestimable influence on the manner in which many Gentile Christians interpreted the Old Testament.

Other second century writings show how many practices and doctrines of the first Christians were undergoing substantial changes. The earliest Christians observed the seventh day Sabbath, whereas many now observed the "eighth day." The first Christians read the Old Testament as literal instructions from God, accepting limited allegorical applications. Now some individuals believed that God never intended the teachings given to ancient Israel to be taken literally. The Jewish roots of the apostles' epistles were being replaced by new writings that were decidedly Hellenistic and anti-Jewish.

The Spread of Gnosticism

During the second century a religion, now called Gnosticism by scholars, began to gain popularity. Many adherents claimed their beliefs to be the authentic Christianity.

Two Gnostic leaders of the late first century are worth mentioning. They were partly responsible for the spread of Docetism—the belief that Jesus didn't exist in a real body, but only appeared to be human. One was Menander, a Samaritan like Simon the Magician. The other was Cerinthus, who taught in Asia Minor. According to Irenaeus, the Apostle John came across Cerinthus in a public bathhouse and fled saying, "Let us get out of here, for fear that the place falls in, now that Cerinthus, the enemy of the truth, is inside."[18]

An early second century Gnostic named Valentinus gained substantial success in promoting his brand of Gnosticism. Valentinus, like many other Gnostics, mixed his theology with Platonic philosophy. Plato taught that there are two realms of existence—mind and matter. In the realm of mind, or spirit, there are ideals, or archetypes. Objects in the material realm are just copies of the ideals. Plato called the creator god the *demiurge* (craftsman). Matter eternally existed in a state of chaos, but the *demiurge* created imperfect objects based on the ideals.[19]

Gnostics educated in Greek philosophy began to draw parallels between Plato's spiritual ideals and imperfect material objects on the one hand, and the concepts of good and evil on the other. They concluded that matter was evil. This belief that matter was evil led to the conclusion that Jesus Christ, as the perfect Son of God, could not have actually become flesh. Instead, he must have appeared to be human.

Plato's *demiurge* came to be seen as *Yahweh* of the Old Testament, who was an inferior God, or even an angel, and not the supreme god. Therefore, the laws given by the God of the Old Testament to ancient Israel were flawed. Jesus came to reveal a greater God and to free human beings from the inferior teachings of the Old Testament.

These teachings inspired some Gnostic groups to lives of debauchery. One Gnostic sect, led by Carpocrates, concluded that since all matter is worthless, a truly spiritual person should abandon himself to every lust. They believed that good and evil were human inventions, and that through reincarnation all people were to experience "every kind of life."[20]

The Cainites taught that Cain was the real hero of the biblical story, as were Esau, Korah and the Sodomites. The Cainites also believed that Judas was the one disciple who truly understood Jesus and they put stock in the teachings of the *Gospel of Judas*.[21] Other Gnostics took the opposite view, teaching that since matter was evil, the pinnacle of a moral life is the pursuit of asceticism.

The Greek idea of both the preexistence and immortality of the soul is reflected in the Gnostic book *The Exegesis of the Soul*. In this strange mixture of sexual allegory and quotes from both the Bible and Homer's *Odyssey*, the soul, who is female, sins against her father and descends into a body. When the soul desires to return to the father, she repents and is baptized. *The Exegesis of the Soul* states, "And so the cleansing of the soul is to regain the [newness] of her former nature and to turn herself back again. That is her baptism."[22]

Riding a growing tide of anti-Jewish sentiment throughout many quarters of the empire, and appealing to Hellenistic culture, Gnosticism threatened to become the dominant form of Christianity.

Ebionites and Marcionites

The confusion and diversity of Christianity in the second century is illustrated in the teachings of two groups—the Ebionites and the Marcionites.

The Ebionites were a Jewish Christian group who tried to maintain practices found in the Old Testament. They kept the seventh-day Sabbath, adhered to laws concerning clean and unclean meats, and required circumcision. They accepted Jesus as the Messiah, but denied His divinity. Jesus was seen as a created human being, although he was accepted as a unique man in his relationship with God. They saw in his death the perfect sacrifice for sin, and taught that there was no longer a need for animal sacrifices.[23]

On the other end of the biblical interpretation scale were the Gnostic Marcionites. Marcion arrived in Rome around 140 and was excommunicated by the Roman church in 144. For Marcion, the differences between the God revealed in the Old Testament and the God revealed in the New Testament were so contradictory that he concluded they must be two different gods. He taught that the God of the Old Testament was the Creator God who emphasized justice, while Jesus came to reveal the supreme god, who was a being of love and grace.

Henry Chadwick writes in *The Early Church*, "The God of the Jews, Marcion argued, was vacillating: after forbidding the making of images, he told Moses to set up a brazen serpent. He was ignorant: he had to ask Adam where he was and descended to Sodom and Gomorrah to discover what was going on. Moreover, as the creator of Adam he was responsible for the entrance of evil into the world. In one text of the Old Testament God himself confesses, 'I create evil.' It was congruous, thought Marcion, that he would so favour that bloodthirsty and licentious bandit, King David. Moreover, it was this creator who devised the humiliating method of sexual reproduction...." Marcion was also disgusted by the idea that God would favor the Jewish people.[24]

For Marcion the Old Testament was non-applicable for Christians, as was most of the New Testament. His canon included a highly edited version of Luke's gospel and 10 of Paul's letters. Marcion believed that everything Jewish was a product of the inferior Creator God and had to be eliminated from Christian teachings. He declared that the followers of the Old Testament

God, including Noah and Abraham, were excluded from salvation through Christ.[25]

British historian Paul Johnson in *A History of Christianity* paints Marcion as an individual who "represents two important and permanent strains in Christianity: the cool, rationalist approach to the examination of the Church's documentary proofs, and a plain, unspectacular philosophy of love.... Marcion had no doubt that Paul's essential teachings were sound and he knew that they were closest to Jesus in date. His difficulty was how to square them with either the teachings of the Old Testament, or with post-Pauline Christian writings. Using historical and critical methods similar to those of modern scriptural scholars, he identified only seven Pauline epistles as authentic.... His textual analysis and the process by which he arrived at the first 'canon' thus had a unity: the breach with Judaism, initiated by Paul, had to be complete, and Christian texts with Judaizing tendencies or compromises expurgated or scrapped."[26]

The Ebionites were to have little influence on the development of Christian orthodoxy, while the Marcionites, and other Gnostic groups, were to be major movements for many decades. Their impact is still felt in some quarters of 21st century Christianity.

Drifting Apart

Hadrian's reaction to the Bar Kokhba Revolt was to try to remove all vestiges of the people of Israel from their land. Jewish captives were sold as slaves. The emperor issued edicts making it illegal to study the *Torah*, to observe the Sabbath, or to practice circumcision. Jews were not even allowed to enter the new Roman Jerusalem.[28] Jewish-Christian bishops and parishioners in Jerusalem were removed from the city, and the congregation became composed entirely of Gentiles.[29]

This animosity against anything deemed Jewish was also growing among many Gentile Christian congregations. The *Epistle of Barnabas*, probably written shortly before the Bar

The Infancy Gospel of Thomas

A book that appeared in the second century was the *Infancy Gospel of Thomas*. In this fictional account, a five-year-old Jesus creates sparrows from mud on the Sabbath. A mean-spirited Jesus cripples a child who displeases him and kills another child who runs into him. When some parents complain, Jesus strikes them blind. On another occasion, a child falls from a rooftop and dies. Some people accuse Jesus of pushing him. The Jesus child proves them wrong by resurrecting the dead boy. The book ends with a retelling of the biblical account of Jesus teaching in the temple at age 12.[27]

Kokhba Revolt, shows the emergence of a "Gentile Christianity" disavowing the Israelites as the people of God.

Because of the popularity of writings like the *Epistle of Barnabas*, we can see that prejudice against the Jews as the elect of God wasn't unique to Gnostics like Marcion. In fact, the crack between Christians and Jews, which started in the day of the Apostle Paul, was eroding into a chasm beyond repair. The result was the formation of a new Hellenized Christianity that was in many ways in opposition to the Old Testament and the original teachings of Primitive Christianity.

14

THE EIGHTH DAY AND QUARTODECIMANS

Christians of the first three centuries didn't meet in ornate cathedrals or massive auditoriums. In the early days, the followers of Jesus found their most fertile ground for raising converts from the Jews, proselytes and God-fearers of the Jewish synagogues. Soon pagans began to respond. When driven from the synagogues, Christians met in believers' houses, or even out in the countryside. As the number of converts grew, congregations needed leadership and elders were ordained as teachers and administrators.[1]

A letter from Pliny to Emperor Trajan, written early in the second century, describes Christian services as hymn singing and moral teaching.[2] Justin Martyr describes a service around 150. In that service Christians met on Sundays to partake of the Eucharist and to pray together. He gives this reason for Sunday observance: "But Sunday is the day on which we all hold our common assembly, because it is the first day on which God, having wrought a change in the darkness and matter, made the world; and Jesus Christ our Saviour on the same day rose from the dead. For He was crucified on the day before that of Saturn (Saturday); and on the day after that of Saturn, which is the day of the Sun, having appeared to His apostles and disciples, He taught them these things...."[3]

Through the decades, some congregations began meeting in buildings specifically designed as places of worship. An example of one these early "house churches," built around 232, has been discovered in Syria. It was larger than the average house. The main room could hold around 100 people. The walls were decorated with colorful murals of biblical scenes.[4] During the various imperial persecutions, many of these buildings were seized by the Roman government, forcing Christians to meet in secret. In 313 Emperor Constantine ordered that all Christian buildings be given to the "Catholic Church."[5]

The Eighth Day

The earliest Christians observed the seventh-day Sabbath. By the middle of the second century, many Christians observed Sunday as their day of worship in the belief that Jesus was resurrected on Sunday. The New Testament contains no instructions to observe Sunday as a holy time or day of worship. What happened to cause this transformation?

Justin Martyr taught that God instituted the keeping of the Sabbath for Israel as a sign because of their unrighteousness. It was never intended to be a moral law.[6] He taught that Jewish Sabbath observance was a denial of the New Covenant. The new law required a "perpetual sabbath." He wrote, "if there be any perjured person or a thief among you, let him cease to be so; if any adulterer, let him repent; then he has kept the sweet and true sabbaths of God."[7] Justin agreed to fellowship with Christians who continued to practice circumcision, to observe the Sabbath or to perform other "Jewish" rituals as long as they didn't require other Christians to observe them.[8]

As we have already seen, one catalyst for this transformation was the popularity of the *Epistle of Barnabas*, which taught that the Israelites misinterpreted God's instructions by taking them literally instead of grasping their deeper allegorical meaning. With anti-Jewish sentiment sweeping across many parts of the Roman Empire, both before and after the Bar Kokhba Revolt, many Gentile Christians found the teachings of this epistle appealing.

The letter claimed that the Sabbath established by God at creation wasn't a literal day but a reference to the future 1,000-year reign of Christ. The six days of creation pictured 6,000 years of human history between Adam and the Second Advent. In this present age, people are unholy and therefore unable to observe a holy day. Only after Christ's return can people be holy and experience holy time.

The writer concluded, "It is not the Sabbaths of the present age that are acceptable to me [God], but the one I have made, in which I will give rest to all things and make the beginning of an eighth day, which is the beginning of another world. Therefore, also we celebrate the eighth day with gladness, for on it Jesus arose from the dead, and appeared, and ascended into heaven."[9]

The *Epistle of Barnabas* claimed that God had established a new spiritual meaning in the "eighth day," which fell on the first day of the week. The writer also rejected physical Israel as the people of God and denied the validity of Jewish biblical and historical interpretation.

Justin Martyr in his *Dialogue with Trypho* explained that "the eighth day possessed a certain mysterious import, which the seventh day did not possess, and which was promulgated by God through these rites."[10] Further proof of the "mysterious import" was the fact that God saved eight people on Noah's ark, signifying the relationship between the number eight and salvation. Justin believed that God's instruction for Jews to circumcise their baby boys on the eighth day was a literal command picturing the future

Christian circumcision of the heart, celebrated on Sunday, the new eighth day.[11]

Clement of Alexandria, writing toward the end of the second century, went as far as to claim that in *The Republic* Plato had prophesied the significance of the Christian eighth day.[12]

The "eighth day" reasoning that helped lead Christians away from the Sabbath of the Ten Commandments had no basis in Old Testament teachings, or in the practices and teachings of Jesus or his apostles.

These writers lived in a time when Gnosticism threatened to become the dominate form of Christianity. Both Justin Martyr and Clement of Alexandria fought against the Gnostics, yet they had some things in common with their enemies: mainly a deep-seated anti-Jewish sentiment and a Greek philosophical approach to biblical interpretation. Gnostics like Marcion, or popular writings like the *Epistle of Barnabas*, sprang from the same Hellenistic melting pot. This Hellenistic spirit continues to guide much Christian thought today.

The Passover/Easter Controversy

Another major controversy arose in the second century among Christian groups. This debate centered on whether Christians should observe Passover or Easter. The earliest Christians had observed the Passover. A leading bishop in Asia Minor named Polycarp (c. 60-156), who had been one of the disciples of the Apostle John, followed in his mentor's footsteps by observing Passover on the 14th day of the first month of the Hebrew calendar. In contrast, the church at Rome adopted the practice of observing Easter Sunday.

Polycarp confronted the Roman bishop Anicetus, who held his office from 154-168, concerning the Passover/Easter controversy. Polycarp argued that by observing the Passover on Abib 14 he was following the teachings of John. Anicetus said that he must follow the customs of his parishioners. The two agreed to part in peace.[13]

A copy of a letter from Polycarp to the Philippians survives. In the letter, he instructs them to live moral lives in accordance with the "Divine commandments" and to follow the example of Jesus. Polycarp also condemns Docetism.[14]

According to one account, Polycarp was later killed in the arena in Smyrna. When soldiers tried to burn him at the stake, his body wouldn't burn. A solider then stabbed him and he died quickly.[15]

In Asia Minor, Polycrates succeeded Polycarp. The Passover/Easter controversy again became critical. Christians who observed Passover were called "Quartodecimans," meaning those who observed the 14th of the first month of the Hebrew calendar. During the time of Victor I, who was bishop of Rome from 190-202, Polycrates confronted him about the lack of biblical precedence for Easter observance.

Victor held his ground, arguing that Easter was the custom of the Roman church. He excommunicated all the churches in Asia Minor that insisted on observing the Passover. Easter was declared the official Christian observance in the West. The bishop of Rome was becoming a powerful force.

Since the apostles never taught Easter observance, and there are no cases of Christians observing Easter in the New Testament, the claim by Roman bishops that they were following the earliest teachings was unfounded.[16]

Henry Chadwick concludes in *The Early Church*, "It was impossible in so weighty a practical question for diversity to be allowed, but there can be little doubt that the Quartodecimans were right in thinking that they had preserved the most ancient and apostolic custom. They had become heretics simply by being behind the times."[17] Christianity was evolving and those who followed the teachings of the earliest apostles were losing the debate.

Polycrates' Letter to Victor I

In a passionate letter Polycrates defended his Passover observance to Victor: "We for our part keep the day scrupulously, without addition or subtraction. For in Asia great luminaries sleep who shall rise again on the day of the Lord's advent, when He is coming with glory from heaven and shall search out all His saints—such as Philip, one of the twelve apostles, who sleeps in Hierapolis with two of his daughters, who remained unmarried to the end of their days, while his other daughter lived in the Holy Spirit and rests in Ephesus." He supported his position by claiming that the Apostle John, who "also sleeps in Ephesus," as well as Polycarp and a number of other prominent church leaders, observed the Passover on Abib 14. Among the other leaders was Melito, "who lies in Sardis waiting for the visitation from heaven when he shall rise from the dead...."

He continued: "All of these kept the fourteenth day of the month as the beginning of the Paschal festival, in accordance with the Gospel, not deviating in the least but following the rule of the Faith. Last of all I too, Polycrates, the least of you all, act according to the tradition of my family, some members I have actually followed; for seven of them were bishops and I am the eighth, and my family have always kept the day when people put away leaven. So I, my friends, after spending sixty-five years in the Lord's service and conversing with Christians from all parts of the world, and going carefully through all Holy Scripture, am not scared of threats. Better people than I have said, 'We must obey God rather than men.'"[18]

The fact that these Christians observed Abib 14 as the beginning of the "Paschal festival" implies the observance of the entire Feast of Unleavened Bread. It is also important to notice that Polycrates is promoting the early Christian teaching that the dead are asleep, "waiting for the visitation from heaven when they shall rise from the dead...."

The Challenges Continue

One hundred years after the death of the Apostle John, Christianity was developing into a conflicting mixture of competing doctrines and practices. The first century controversies over issues of Jewish sectarianism and circumcision were replaced by battles with Gnosticism, Hellenism and paganism. For many Christians the Hebrew Scriptures no longer supplied literal instructions from God, as it did for Jesus' earliest disciples, but were seen as allegorical teachings or even irrelevant to Gentile believers. Jerusalem was no longer the center of ecclesiastical authority.

W.H.C. Frend in *The Rise of Christianity* sums up the period between the second fall of Jerusalem in 135 and the end of the second century as witnessing "...great changes in the organization of the church and the outlook of its members. At the beginning of this period, many Christians were still nonconformist Jews. In asserting that Jesus was the Messiah and that the prophecies of the Old Testament referred to him alone, they might incur the enmity of the orthodox Jews, but their tenacity of purpose and total rejection of idolatry, including the imperial cult, would have done credit to the Essenes."[19] Amid the confusion a new Hellenistic orthodoxy was forming.

Adding to the confusion was that in different parts of the empire Christians were dragged into the arena and crucified, burned at the stake or thrown to wild animals. During the second and third centuries officials of the empire often claimed Christians were atheists, or charged them with committing a variety of criminal acts—even human sacrifice.[20] The catacombs of Rome, a vast underground city extending hundreds of miles through the drainage and sewage system, contain hundreds of inscriptions from Christians fleeing persecution. Although some Christians recanted, returning to paganism, many were killed for their beliefs. In this sometimes hostile environment, Christianity continued to remain a minority religion, despised as a "wicked superstition."[21]

15

HELLENIZED ORTHODOXY

In 331 BC Alexander the Great supervised the surveying of a new port city he envisioned on the Egyptian shore of the Mediterranean Sea. The lines for streets and buildings were laid out using barley flour. A few days later, Alexander embarked on other adventures, leaving behind the groundwork of the city that would bear his name—Alexandria.[1] By the time Julius Caesar marched into town, Alexandria housed the greatest library and museum in the ancient world. It was the intellectual capital of antiquity.

The Rise and Fall of Alexandria: Birthplace of the Modern World captures the wonder of the city: "Within a few generations of its foundation the city was the marvel of its age, but not just for its size and beauty, its vast palaces, safe harbors, and fabled lighthouse [one of the seven wonders of the ancient world], or even for being the world's greatest emporium, its central market. Alexandria was built on knowledge..."[2]

The Ptolemaic rulers transformed Alexander's port into the center of Hellenistic culture. Here the ideas of Plato and Aristotle were discussed by philosophers from all over the Mediterranean. The study of science, mechanics, mathematics and geography flourished in an environment that promoted intellectual freedom and multiculturalism. In many ways it outshone Athens as the model of Hellenistic culture.

Alexandria supported a large Jewish population. In the first century its most famous Jewish citizen was Philo, who attempted to merge Hebrew Scripture with Greek Culture. W.H.C. Frend paints this picture of Philo in *The Rise of Christianity*: "He was Greek to the core, in language, education, and manners, and his Bible was the Septuagint. For him there was no incompatibility between Hellenism and Judaism. While accepting the Law as the infallibly revealed will of God to both Jews and Gentiles, he attempted to interpret it exclusively through the mirror of Greek philosophy."[3]

It isn't surprising that during the second century Gnosticism found fertile ground in Alexandria. Gnostic teachers like Valentinus and Basilides and their disciples taught that the Old Testament law was the product of a lesser god. A person could be freed from the law through the *gnosis* sent by God in Christ. Through gnosis a person's soul could obtain liberty and eventually return to its heavenly home.

These Gnostic teachers denied the actual death of Jesus as a sacrifice. Basilides taught that before his crucifixion, Jesus exchanged souls with Simon of Cyrene. The unsuspecting Jew found himself inhabiting Jesus' crucified body while the real Jesus stood by and laughed.

The Alexandrian Gnostics adopted ideas from both Plato and Philo. They concluded that the Old Testament was not to be read as an historical document, but as allegories of the mysteries of Christian *gnosis*. The Jews were despised as people who followed a lesser God rather than the one revealed by Christ.[4]

The philosophical climate of the city that prided itself in being the center of all knowledge, and a city where Hellenized Judaism and Gnosticism flourished, was fertile ground for the formation of Hellenized Christian orthodoxy.

Neo-Platonism

In the third century a number of philosophers attempted to revive Platonic teachings, resulting in the movement known as Neo-Platonism. This movement found its epicenter in Alexandria.

The most influential of the early Neo-Platonists was Plotinus (c. 204-269). Plotinus described God as "the One" who transcended all matter, but was impersonal to humans. All souls were at one time with God, but because of a desire for independence, many souls descended into the physical realm to become human beings. Through a life of asceticism, humans could be freed from the present state and return to an ecstatic relationship with God.[5]

Alexandrian Hellenistic Christianity

Two men stand out among the Neo-Platonist theologians who were influential in forming Hellenistic Christian orthodoxy—Clement of Alexandria (c. 153-217) and Origin (c. 185-254).

Clement saw Greek philosophy as a schoolmaster to bring the "Hellenic mind" to Christ much the same way Paul said the Law was given to bring Jews to Christ. "Accordingly, before the advent of the Lord, philosophy was necessary to the Greeks for righteousness."[6] He concluded that "Greek preparatory culture, therefore, with philosophy itself, is shown to have come down from God to men, not with a definite direction, but in the way in which showers fall down on the good land, and on the dunghill, and on the houses."[7] Clement promoted the study of Greek philosophies in order to dig out the nuggets of truth.

For Clement, the reason Plato had discovered so much of the truth about the nature of God and moral law was due to his familiarity with the writings of Moses. Greek philosophy may be theologically flawed, but in Clements' view its concepts were imbued with divine inspiration and insight linked directly to the Law.[8]

Clements' most famous pupil was Origen. Origen was a prolific writer who is considered one of the greatest scholars of the first Christian centuries. Although Origen was critical of Greek philosophers, he was strongly influenced by Neo-Platonism.

Origen taught that the God of the Bible was the Creator of all things. Unlike Plato, he believed that matter wasn't eternal but was created by God. God also created a host of living souls who preexisted with him before the creation of the universe. Some souls rebelled against God and became Satan and the demons, while others lost their unity with God and became heavenly forms like the sun, moon or stars, or were encased in human bodies.[9] He also taught that humans live in physical bodies to experience a time of testing and teaching in order to return to their original state. Eventually, God would bring all souls back into a heavenly unity and all things would be as they were in the beginning.[10]

For Origen, the Bible was to be explored as an allegory of hidden truth. Origen concluded that since New Testament writers mention "one Israel according to the flesh, and another according to the Spirit," and Paul writes of a "heavenly Jerusalem," then all passages in the Old and New Testaments mentioning Israel, Judah or Jerusalem were to be understood as allegories concerning Christians and the Church.[11] The Church is the true people of God and the promises made to Israel in the Old Testament no longer apply to Jews since they are no longer the people of God.

His trinity doctrine stated that the Son and Holy Spirit were subordinate to the Father. This subordination didn't relegate the

Son to being a created being. The Father-Son relationship was eternal and an essential aspect of God's nature.[12]

Origen's zeal was such that when he read Jesus' instructions, "and there are eunuchs who have made themselves eunuchs for the kingdom of heaven's sake," he took the words literally and mutilated himself.[13] Later Catholic scholars would condemn some of Origin's teachings, but his impact on the development of Christianity can't be underestimated.

Tertullian

The theologians from the school in Alexandria weren't the only ones involved in the development of Hellenized orthodoxy. Tertullian (c. 160-220), the first major author to present Christian ideas in Latin, is considered one of the founders of Latin Christianity. He hailed from Carthage in North Africa, having converted from a pagan background. Tertullian published many works, including *The Apology*, a defense of Christian teachings, and five books debunking the heresies of Marcion.

In addition to works defending the need for repentance and water baptism, he was the first writer to describe the doctrine of the trinity in Latin terms that would form the foundation of later Catholic teachings. Admitting that the majority of Christians were "startled" by his "Three in One" explanation of the Godhead, Tertullian taught that the Father, Son and Holy Spirit are not the same "Person," but are "of one substance, and of one condition, and of one power."[14]

Tertullian held to the Greek concept that all the dead go to *Hades*, a place deep inside the earth where there are two regions, one for the evil and one for the good. The righteous consciously wait for the resurrection to occur at Christ's return. The only exceptions were Christian martyrs put into a special "reception room" that was "under the altar"—a reference to the Apostle John's vision in Revelation.[15]

In *The Apology*, Tertullian chided Christians for participating in pagan celebrations such as Saturnalia. He also quoted the Old Testament prophet Isaiah to condemn Jewish holy days and the seventh-day Sabbath. Tertullian claimed that for Christians, the Jewish "Sabbaths are strange." He argued that it is pagan celebrations that occur annually, but that Christians "have a festive day every eighth day."[16] The "eighth day" teaching found in the *Epistle of Barnabas* forgery had become the standard Christian explanation for worshipping on Sunday.

Later in his life Tertullian became a Montanist. Members of this movement claimed to be special mouthpieces of the Holy Spirit. They prophesied the imminent return of Jesus Christ, promoted speaking in tongues, accentuated asceticism, and extolled the advantages of suffering a martyr's death. The Asian bishops convened their first church synods to excommunicate the Montanists.[17]

The Roman World and Christianity in the Third Century

The popular philosophy of Stoicism both rivaled Hellenistic Christianity and helped its growth. Educated people were attracted to Stoicism because of its teachings about one god and because of its pursuit of virtue. Stoicism reached its peak of influence with the reign of Marcus Aurelius (161-180). His book *Meditations* is the personal deliberations of a man of power trying to live by Stoic virtues. After his death in 180, Aurelius was followed by his son Commodus, whose rule was marked by ineptness and debauchery. When Commodus was assassinated, army officers literally auctioned off the most powerful office in the world to the highest bidder.

A general from North Africa named Septimius Severus marched on Rome and restored order. From 193 to 235 members of the Severus family ruled the empire. Their reign would be known as the Severan dynasty.[18]

After the Severan dynasty the empire fell into difficult times.

For almost 50 years the empire suffered almost constant warfare from barbarian and Parthian incursions as well as from internal strife. Entire provinces were overrun, and cities such as Athens besieged. Inflation devalued coinage. Emperors came and went with destabilizing frequency. In numerous cities public buildings and aqueducts fell into disrepair while epidemics and famines ravished various regions of the empire.[19]

During this period, and continuing into the next century, official Roman persecution of Christians flared and ebbed, but never completely died-out. There were severe persecutions during the reigns of Marcus Aurelius, Decius (249-238) and Valerian (253-260). Diocletian (284-305) attempted to eradicate all groups that declared themselves Christian.

In spite of persecution, competition with other Christian sects, and continued battles with Gnosticism throughout the third century, Hellenized Christian orthodoxy gained a strong foothold. This doesn't mean that Hellenized orthodoxy was a monolithic movement. Theologians argued over the nature of Jesus Christ, church discipline and baptism. The Quartodeciman controversy erupted again in mid century, but the Easter faction once again carried the day.[20]

Drifting from the moorings of a literal understanding of the Old Testament, and distancing itself from any association with Jews, the new orthodoxy was becoming universal in appeal. Pagans were converting to Hellenized Christianity through the syncretism of the Bible with Greek philosophy. W.H.C. Frend points out, "For two centuries the relationship between Platonism and Christianity oscillated between attraction and repulsion. Basically, nothing could be more opposed than the Jewish and Greek view of God, of creation, of time and history, and of the role of humanity in the universe." This had changed. In Alexandria, the works of Philo, Alexandrian Gnostics, Clement and Origen all combined to produce a pagan-friendly biblical interpretation seen through a Platonic lens.[21]

With his teachings concerning the preexistence of the soul, Origen tied Christian arguments to Platonism. Tertullian's two compartments in *Hades* were recognizable to the Greek world. The trinity doctrine espoused by Tertullian and others was winning the intellectual battle with the Gnostic teaching of multiple gods. Throughout a time of persecution, economic distress, plagues and war, Hellenized Christianity became a major influence in the Roman world.

Manichaeism and Mithraism

Roman multiculturalism created an environment in which new religious movements could emerge and swiftly gain popularity. One group that flourished was founded by a Persian named Mani (c. 216-276). It sought to bring many religious teachings into one central system. The new religion combined paganism from Persia and Babylon as well as elements of Buddhism, the Bible and Gnosticism. The followers of Mani claimed to have the true *gnosis* that led to salvation. Manichaeism experienced amazing growth during the third century.

Mani launched his ministry in Babylon by proclaiming, "As once Buddha came to India, Zoroaster to Persia, and Jesus to the lands of the West, so came in the present time this Prophecy through me..."[22] He taught that before the universe was created, two "Principles" existed. The Good Principle, known as the Father of Majesty, dwelt in light. The Bad Principle, known as the Prince of Darkness, or Satan, dwelt in darkness.

The Prince of Darkness invaded the kingdom of light, launching the battle between good and evil. The Manicheans believed in a complicated mythology to explain this continuing warfare. Human beings were one of the Father's creations in his battle with the Prince of Darkness.

Manicheans divided humans into three types: "the Perfect, the Hearers and the Sinners (non-Manichaeans)." Upon death the souls of the Perfect were accepted immediately by Jesus into heaven. The souls of the Hearers were relegated to purgatory where they were purified and eventually entered heaven. The souls of Sinners were sent to hell to suffer eternal torment.[23]

While Manichean teachings gained popularity, another pagan religion gained even greater status throughout the empire. It was the worship of a god from the East called Mithra. In Mithraism the highest god was "Infinite Time." As the sun-god, Mithra was the god of light and preeminent among the planetary beings.

Mithraism taught that the souls of human beings were created together and each one passed through the seven planets (who were living beings), where they received their individual traits. Mithra was humanity's savior and mediator between the highest god and man. He was often portrayed as fighting a bull—picturing the human struggles of life. Upon death, the immortal souls of sinners were condemned to hell, but the souls of those who worshipped Mithra passed through the "spheres of the seven planets." At the end of this purifying process they were allowed to live for eternity with the highest god.

Worshippers underwent seven degrees of initiation: crow, occult, soldier, lion, Persian, solar messenger and father. Each stage had its own standards of dress and rituals. Rituals were elaborate, but being a mystery religion, few details of how worship ceremonies were conducted have survived. It is known that worshippers often met in caves to eat a sacred meal of bread and either juice or wine. They prayed three times a day towards the sun, and Sunday was the official day of worship. December 25th was observed as Mithra's birthday to celebrate the renewal of the winter sun.

Mithraism excluded females from the cult, promoted strict asceticism, and emphasized manhood and bravery. Because of these traits the cult was very popular in the ranks of the Roman army.[24] Strangely, in the next century the Roman army was to play a part in propelling Hellenized Christian orthodoxy toward prominence as the official religion of the empire, and elements of Mithraism would be added to the syncretism.

16

HELLENIZED
CHRISTIANITY
TRIUMPHANT

In 311 Rome was once again engaged in a bloody civil war. About two miles north of Rome, at the site of the Milvian Bridge over the Tiber River, the forces of Maxentius squared off against the army of Constantine. Thousands of men slashed and stabbed each other to determine the fate of the empire. Maxentius' left flank caved-in. His soldiers panicked and tried to make it to the safety of Rome's walls by crossing the Tiber on a wooden-boat bridge. The bridge collapsed and many soldiers, including their general, drowned.[1]

More than a few soldiers in Constantine's army believed this victory was pre-ordained. They knew their trusted general as a man who received supernatural visions. The accounts of what happened the morning before the Battle of Milvian Bridge are muddled. By one account, Constantine saw a cross in the sky with a Latin phrase that led him to believe that Christ was going to lead him to victory. Another explanation is that during the night he had a dream and the next day it was interpreted to mean that the

Christ was with him. Whatever the case, that morning his soldiers marched against the legions of Maxentius under a new banner—the sign of the cross and the Latin inscription *Chi-Rho*.[2]

Generations of Christians would see this sign as a defining moment—the time when the resurrected Christ became directly involved with Western civilization. The reality had more to do with practical politics. At the time, the *Chi-Rho* symbol was not a well-known Christian emblem. In fact, it may have been associated more with Apollo or Mithra. Michael Grant in *Constantine the Great* concludes that "the Christogram could be reverenced by both pagans and Christians: an illustration of Constantine's desire to play to both audiences."[3]

Constantine publicly proclaimed his victory was a gift from the Christian God and then declared himself a Christian, though he wasn't baptized until just before his death. The *Encyclopedia Britannica* states that "the notion of a conversion in the sense of a real acceptance of the new religion, and a thorough rejection of the old, is inconsistent with the hesitating attitude in which he stood towards both. Much of this may indeed be due to motives of political expediency, but there is a good deal that cannot be so explained. Paganism must still have been an operative belief in the man who, down almost to the close of his life, retained so many pagan superstitions. He was at best only half heathen, half Christian, who could seek to combine the worship of Christ with the worship of Apollo, having the name of one and the figure of the other impressed on his coins, and ordaining the observance of Sunday under the name *Dies Solis* [the Sun god] in his celebrated decree of March, 321, though such a combination was far from uncommon in the first Christian centuries."[4]

Constantine was a man of his times. He may have been "half heathen, half Christian," but the same could be said of the Hellenized Christianity he accepted. During his reign he improved the physical infrastructure throughout the empire; pursued economic policies that created inflation; and legalized

Christianity. Also, in typical fashion for Roman emperors, he murdered members of his own family.

Even as a co-ruler before the civil war, Constantine was instrumental in issuing edicts giving legal status to the Christian religion. These privileges increased after he was made sole emperor. He gave property rights to the "Catholic"[5] or universal church. He commanded bishops to hold synods in order to settle theological and administrative differences. In one letter, Constantine chastised bishops who were "creating divisions regarding the worship of the holy and heavenly Power and the Catholic Religion..." and ordered a synod to resolve the conflict.[6] In another edict the Christian clergy were declared free from public duties.[7]

On March 7, 321 he issued one of his most famous edicts: "All judges, city-people and craftsmen shall rest on the venerable day of the Sun. But countrymen may without hindrance attend to agriculture, since it often happens that this is the most suitable day for sowing grain or planting vines, so that the opportunity afforded by divine providence may not be lost, for the right season is of short duration."[8]

In July of the same year the emperor declared, "Just as we thought it most unfitting that the day of the Sun, with its venerable rites, should be given over to the swearing and counter-swearing of litigants and their unseemly brawls, so it is a pleasant and joyful thing to fulfill petitions of special urgency on that day. Therefore on that festal day let all be allowed to perform manumission and emancipation; and let nothing that concerns this be forbidden."[9] Sunday became the official day of "venerable rites" throughout the Roman Empire.

Constantine would wield powerful influence over the formation of church doctrine as he helped shape Hellenized orthodoxy into a Catholic faith. For this undertaking, history would crown him Constantine the Great.

An honest question remains for Christians of the 21st century who are the heirs of Constantine's influences: How different was the Hellenized Christianity of Constantine's time compared to Primitive Christianity of the first century?[10] We must also ask ourselves, how much is Christianity of the 21st century a product of Hellenistic syncretism compared to the faith once delivered by Jesus and lived by his first followers?

Primitive Christianity and Hellenized Christianity

It is commonly accepted that the evolution from a Christian religion rooted in the Hebrew Scriptures and teachings of Jesus to a religion molded by Platonic philosophy was a natural result of the teachings of the Apostle Paul. Paul Johnson in *A History of Christianity* summarizes the view that Paul led a Christian revolution away from any real connection with Judaism: "Paul's gospel, as it evolved, could be seen to be alien to traditional Jewish thinking of any tendency, even though it contained Jewish elements.... It is cosmic and universalist; in fact, Hellenized—Paul the Jew, whose natural tongue was Aramaic and whose Greek was singular, had supplied the part of the Hellenized processing machine, and thus made Judaic monotheism accessible to the entire Roman world."[11]

Was Paul's break with the Old Testament as complete as ancient Gnostics, Hellenists or many modern Christians believe? It's time for Christians to return to their biblical roots. Let's look at a few major teachings of the primitive church that were changed due to Hellenistic influences and are still reflected today in the tenets of many modern denominations.

- Primitive Christians emphasized continuity between the Old and New Testaments.

  A study of the New Testament shows that for the earliest Christians the people and events of the Hebrew Scriptures were seen as historically accurate accounts of God's interaction with human beings. The New Testament writers quoted extensively from the Old Testament as support for doctrines and practices. Hellenized Gentiles found the idea of Jewish election repugnant and they either attempted to allegorize the Old Testament or lay claim that the promises made to ancient Israel now applied in a spiritual sense to the Church. The effect was to create a theological method for abrogating any Old Testament teaching the Hellenists deemed undesirable.

- Primitive Christians understood Jesus as the Messiah in the context of the Old Testament prophecies. Consequently, they understood his past, present and future roles (Savior, High Priest, and Messianic King) not only as fulfilling the promises to Abraham's physical descendants, but also as roles through which he brings all people to God.

- Primitive Christians taught that being baptized and receiving the Holy Spirit are the signs of the New Covenant, and therefore necessary to the salvation process.

  For the earliest Christians, baptism was more than a ritualistic profession of faith that magically guaranteed salvation. Before baptism new converts were to repent of their sins and dedicate their lives in obedience to God. Baptism and the laying on of hands to receive the Holy Spirit were seen as outward signs of participating in the New Covenant. Converts then entered the *ecclesia*, in which they were expected to remain faithful to the covenant. True Christianity involved a complete change of mind, heart and actions.

- Primitive Christians taught that the Spirit of the Ten Commandments didn't eliminate the need to observe the letter of the Ten Commandments.

A primary issue in Paul's writings is justification. Paul wanted Christians to understand that no human being, Gentile or Jew, could make himself righteous enough to earn a relationship with God. God's law defines good and evil conduct. The rituals of the Old Covenant did not make anyone righteous, but instead provided a way for sinful men to express repentance and to offer worship. The dilemma was that the *Torah* could not offer eternal salvation to anyone who had broken the law. Paul was adamant that "the Scripture has defined all under sin."[12]

The problem he addressed is how God could supply forgiveness to a sinful humanity without compromising with his righteousness and justice? How could a sinful person be given the privilege to enter into a relationship with God, thereby receiving the opportunity for eternal salvation?

In his Epistle to the Galatians, Paul dealt with Christians who tried to persuade Gentiles to be circumcised and to become full Jewish proselytes as a means to salvation. Paul was unyielding in teaching that no one, Jew or Gentile, could be declared righteous before God simply through law-keeping or accumulating good works. He wrote: "We who are Jews by nature, and not sinners of the Gentiles, knowing that a man is not justified by the works of the law but by faith in Jesus Christ...." He also wrote that "by the works of the law no flesh shall be justified."[13]

He later wrote that God's forgiveness, and the privilege of a relationship with God, can't be earned by human works. It is available only to those who have faith in the redemptive work of Jesus Christ.[14] Only through accepting the substitute sacrifice of the Son of God can human beings receive the forgiveness that allows them to be declared righteous and therefore able to approach the omnipotent Lawgiver.

The covenant God gave through Moses to Abraham's descendants was a "tutor," the *paidagogos*, to lead them to the Messiah. Those who accepted Jesus as the Messiah no longer needed the tutor because they now related to God as children in his family.[15] Does this mean that Paul considered the law of God void and of no importance to Christians?

Remember, the major controversy of the early Christian decades was whether the followers of Jesus would become a Pharisaical sect or expand to include God-fearers and new pagan converts. The historical accounts in Acts show that Paul never expected Jews who accepted Jesus as the Messiah to give up circumcision, Sabbaths or temple worship, and neither did he expect Gentile converts to adhere to all the rituals of the *Torah* or the oral law. Paul's position with Gentile converts was similar to the Jewish acceptance of God-fearers. These Gentiles obeyed the Ten Commandments and participated in Sabbath synagogue worship, but they did not participate in circumcision, sacrifices or Jewish oral traditions.

Paul introduced Christianity to pagans by teaching that they were not subject to Jewish oral law or to the administration of the Levitical priesthood, but were to obey the law under the administration of Christ. This approach may have seemed radical to Judean Pharisees, but it rang a bell with God-fearers who had converted to Judaism. This is why Paul could write to the Corinthians, "Circumcision is nothing and uncircumcision is nothing, but keeping the commandments of God is what matters."[16]

In 2 Corinthians 3 Paul taught that the laws written on tables of stone, the Ten Commandments, were the same laws written in the hearts of Christians. Could Paul mean that what he calls the "ministry of the Spirit" nullified the need for the followers of Christ to obey the letter of the commandments? Wouldn't it be absurd to argue that it would be acceptable for a man to break the letter of the law by committing adultery, as long as he obeyed the spirit of the commandment by not lusting in his heart? It would be equally absurd to claim that the wife could break the letter of the law by murdering her adulterous husband, but obey the spirit of the law by killing him in love.

Although most modern Christians wouldn't suggest that a person could literally commit murder and still obey the spirit of the law, the early Hellenists accepted the notion that Christians could break the seventh-day Sabbath commandment in the letter as long as they kept a "perpetual Sabbath" by being in a state of worship on all days. Because this interpretation has been accepted in mainstream Christianity for so long, even modern Christians who claim the Ten Commandments are still in effect seldom question why all the commandments except one are to be taken literally.

Irenaeus wrote that the Ten Commandments were God's natural law for all mankind, declaring that "if any one does not observe, he has no salvation."[17] He went on to write, "Preparing man for this life, the Lord himself did speak in His own person to all alike the words of the Decalogue; and therefore, in like manner, do they remain permanently with us, receiving by means of His advent in the flesh, extension and increase, but not abrogation."[18]

He also taught that God gave circumcision and the Sabbaths to Israel as signs that they were his people. For Irenaeus, the Church replaced physical circumcision with the spiritual circumcision of the heart. The seventh-day Sabbath "taught that we should continue day by day in God's service."[19] While it is true that both circumcision and the weekly Sabbath were given as "signs" of the people of Israel, circumcision was never listed as one of the Ten Commandments which Irenaeus accepts as having vital importance for Christians. Paradoxically, Irenaeus had no problem teaching that the Ten Commandments are literal requirements for Christians while nullifying the literal meaning of the fourth commandment.

First century Christians observed the Ten Commandments as laws written in their hearts by the Holy Spirit. It is impossible to keep those laws in the Spirit and disregard them in the letter. Early Hellenists like Irenaeus held this same interpretation, except in the case of the Fourth Commandment. The Sabbath was seen as a mark of a Jew. In the desire of the Hellenists to separate themselves from anything "Jewish," they voided the literal meaning of the law. This inconsistent approach to the Ten Commandments, breaking with the teachings of Primitive Christianity, has been handed down through the centuries as a tenet of mainstream Christianity.

Throughout Paul's writings he consistently restates the last six of the Ten Commandments as basic Christian moral precepts: honor parents; do not murder; do not commit adultery; do not steal; do not lie; do not covet. He is just as adamant in his support of the first commandment to declare the God of Israel as the only true God. His commitment to the commandment against idolatry matches the fanaticism of the strictest Pharisee or Essene. It would have been inconceivable for him to break the third commandment, taking God's name in vain, and the New Testament consistently shows him as a Sabbath keeper in accordance with the Fourth Commandment. It is a mistake to see the Apostle Paul, whose story is told in Acts, or as the writer of the letters to the Corinthians, as the predecessor to the Hellenized religion of Constantine's time.

- Primitive Christians shunned idolatry. It would have been inconceivable to them to accept statues of saints and crucifixes, which became ubiquitous as Christianity became increasingly Hellenized.

- Primitive Christians observed the Passover instead of Easter.

- Primitive Christians denied the concept of the immortal soul and believed that a person entered a state of "sleep" until the resurrection.

The Consolidation of the Hellenized Orthodox Church

These issues meant little to Constantine, who was concerned with holding together an empire facing economic problems; suppressing political rivals; and stopping barbarian incursions. It was good politics to proclaim Sunday as the day of worship. That proclamation pleased worshipers of the sun god as well as Constantine's soldiers who followed Mithra, but it also pleased Hellenized Christians, who viewed Sunday as the "eighth day" and the day of Jesus' resurrection.

Henry Chadwick in *The Early Church* states, "...Constantine was not aware of any mutual exclusiveness between Christianity and the faith in the Unconquerable Sun. The transition from solar monotheism (the most popular form of contemporary paganism) to Christianity was not difficult. In Old Testament prophecy Christ was entitled 'the sun of righteousness.' Clement of Alexandria (c. AD 200) speaks of Christ driving his chariot across the sky like the Sun-god. A tomb mosaic found recently at Rome, probably made early in the fourth century, depicts Christ as the Sun-god mounting the heavens with his chariot. Tertullian says that many pagans imagined the Christians worshipped the sun because they met on Sundays and prayed towards the East."[20]

Constantine's blessing imbued Hellenized Christianity with political power. The emperor took it upon himself to require

Catholic bishops to unify doctrinal positions. Constantine and subsequent emperors erected ornate cathedrals that rivaled any pagan temple.

However, the rising power of orthodoxy didn't mean the culture of the empire changed overnight. Paganism continued to thrive. Constantine's syncretism played hand-in-hand with trends in local congregations to adopt pagan customs and beliefs. Orthodox Christianity continued to take pagan customs, mold them into a Hellenistic framework, and promote the mixture as an attractive means to make converts.

The result of this religious amalgamation is described by Henry Chadwick: "How easy it was for Christianity and solar religion to become intertwined at the popular level is strikingly illustrated by a mid-fifth century sermon of Pope Leo the Great, rebuking his over-cautious flock for paying reverence to the Sun on the steps of Saint Peter's before turning their back on it to worship inside the westward-facing basilica."[21]

What Does It Matter?

"What does it matter?" you may ask. "All God cares about is that I worship him and try to love my neighbor, right?" The question you should ask instead is, "What was the spiritual way taught by Jesus?"

To find the answers to the spiritual questions of the 21st century we must first return to the original teachings of Jesus and his disciples in the first century. It is time to strip Christianity from Gnostic and Greek influences and return to the "faith once delivered." It won't be easy because Primitive Christianity has been buried by 2,000 years of human traditions.

It is my hope that this short and incomplete overview of how Primitive Christianity became Hellenized will spur individuals who want to live a more pure Christianity to rediscover the original Christians of the New Testament and to follow the real teachings of Jesus Christ.

NOTES

Introduction

(1) Matthew 22:17-21.

1. A Jewish Sect in an Outpost of the Empire

(1) 3 John 9.

(2) *The Annals of Imperial Rome*, Tacitus, Dorsett Press, 1984, p. 365.

(3) Acts 22:22-30; 23:1-35; Acts 26 (notice verses 30-32).

(4) Ezra 1:1-4.

(5) Acts 13:5; 13:14-44; 14:1-7; 17:1-5, 10-13, 16-17; 18:4,8; 19:8.

(6) The Idumeans, or Edomites, are descendants of Esau, the brother of Jacob mentioned in Genesis, and cousins to the Jews.

(7) Herod's killing of Jewish babies is recorded in Matthew 2. When the Roman governor Pontius Pilate sent Jesus to King Agrippa it was because Agrippa was a member of Herod's family and ruled Galilee as a Roman province: Luke 23:6-12.

(8) *Antiquities of the Jews*, Flavius Josephus, Book XIV, ch. X, *Josephus—Complete Works*, translator: William Whiston, Kregel, 1981, pp. 298-302.

(9) *Antiquities of the Jews*, Book XVI, ch. VI, vv. 1-2, p. 344.

(10) *Histories*, Book V, vv. 1-5, Tacitus, Penguin Books, 1993, pp. 279-282.

(11) *Jewish Encyclopedia.com*, article "Seneca, Lucius Annaeus," authors Richard Gottheil and Samuel Krauss.

(12) *The Lives of the Twelve Caesars*, Suetonius, v. 36, The Heritage Press, 1965, p. 181.

(13) Acts 18:2.

(14) The word *Torah* is used to describe Abraham's obedience to God in Genesis 26:5.

(15) *The Interpreter's Dictionary of the Bible* defines *halakhah*: "[from the root 'to walk' with reference to Exodus 18:20].

The authoritative Jewish way of life as expressed in moral law and ritual precept. It embraces the whole body of Jewish teaching, legislation, and practices that proceeded from the interpretation and reinterpretation of the laws of the Bible through an unbroken succession of generations of Jewish teachers from Ezra onward; it also included adaptations or modifications from time to time made applicable to changed conditions of life—economic, domestic, political, social—by spiritual leaders. Although legalistic in content, the Halachah [halakhah] is designed to bring all human occupations into relationship with the service of God and to establish the supremacy of the divine will as the measure of all directions and strivings of human life." (*The Interpreter's Dictionary of the Bible*, Vol. 2, Abington, 1962, article "Halachah" by I. Epstein, p. 512.)

(16) Ezra 7:6,10.

(17) *Abot* 1:1, *The Wisdom of Israel*, Lewis Browne, Random House, 1945, p. 126.

(18) Galatians 1:14. See *Jewish New Testament Commentary*, David H. Stern, Jewish New Testament Publications, Inc., 1994, p, 523-524. Also *Interpreter's Dictionary of the Bible*, Vol. 4, article "Tradition of the Elders" by I.W. Batdorf, Abington Press, 1962, p. 685.

(19) *The Special Laws, IV, The Works of Philo*, v. 150, translator: C.D. Yonge, 1993, p. 631.

2. The God of Abraham, Isaac and Jacob

(1) Genesis 12:1-5.

(2) Genesis 1-3, 6-9; 11:1-9.

(3) Exodus 3.

(4) Exodus 12:37.

(5) Exodus 19-20.

(6) Exodus 20:1-17; Deuteronomy 5:6-21.

(7) Deuteronomy 6:4-5.

(8) Leviticus 19:18.

(9) Deuteronomy 15:1.

(10) Deuteronomy 18:10-11.

(11) Deuteronomy 19:15.

(12) Deuteronomy 22:4.

(13) Deuteronomy 23:19-20.

(14) Deuteronomy 24:19-20.

(15) Leviticus 18:22.

(16) Exodus 20:22-26.

(17) Exodus 32; Numbers 3:5-13; 8:5-22.

(18) Exodus 40:34-38. See *Interpreter's Dictionary of the Bible*, Vol. 4, Abingdon, 1962, article "Shekinah" by D. Moody, pp. 317-319.

(19) 1 Kings 8:1-11.

(20) Examples: Genesis 41:38 (Joseph); Exodus 31:1-6 (artisans for the tabernacle).

(21) Deuteronomy 17:14-20.

(22) Deuteronomy 6:10-16; 12:29-32; 13:1-14.

(23) Deuteronomy 27-30.

(24) Isaiah 2:1-5.

(25) Isaiah 11.

(26) Isaiah 9:6-7.

(27) Isaiah 52:13-53:12.

(28) Daniel 12:1-3.

(29) *The Interpreter's Dictionary of the Bible*, Vol. 4, Abington, 1962, article "Soul," by N.W. Porteous, p. 428. *The Interpreter's Dictionary of the Bible* explains that "...'soul' in English, though it has to some extent naturalized the Hebrew idiom, frequently carries with it overtones, ultimately coming from philosophical Greek (Platonism) and from Orphism and Gnosticism which are absent in nephesh. In the OT it never means the immortal soul, but it is essentially the life principle, or the living being, or the self as the subject of appetite, and emotion, occasionally of volition."

(30) The psalmist writes in Psalm 9:17 that *sheol* is the place where the wicked go upon death. Psalm 88 declares that *sheol*, translated "grave" and "pit," is also the place where the righteous go upon death. *Sheol* is a place of punishment for sin (Proverbs 5:3-

5; Isaiah 5:13-14), and synonymous with being buried in the earth (Job 7:7-10; Job 17:11-16). It is often described as a place of total darkness. Job anguishes, "...before I go to the place from which I shall not return, to the land of darkness and the shadow of death. A land as dark as darkness itself, as the shadows of death without any order, where even the light is like darkness." (Job 10:21-22). Through the prophet Hosea, God declares His ultimate victory over the power of *sheol*: "I will ransom them from the power of the grave; I will redeem them from death. O Death, I will be your plagues! O Grave (*sheol*), I will be your destruction!" (Hosea 13:14).

(31) Psalm 6:5.

(32) Job 14:12-17; Psalm 49:14-15.

(33) Isaiah 26:19.

(34) Ezekiel 37:1-14.

(35) Ezekiel 37:15-28.

(36) *The Jewish Encyclopedia.com* article "Immortality of the Soul," 2002, by Kaufmann Kohler.

(37) *The Interpreter's Dictionary of the Bible*, Vol. 2, Abingdon, 1962, article "Jerusalem," by M. Burrows, pp. 843-844.

(38) Joshua 15:63.

(39) 2 Samuel 5:6-9.

(40) 2 Chronicles 3:1.

(41) Genesis 22:1-2; 2 Samuel 24:18-25.

3. Pythagoras, Plato, Philo and Philosophy

(1) *Classical Greece*, C. M. Bowra, Time Inc., 1965, p. 108.

(2) *The Life of Pythagoras*, Iamblicus, quoted in *The Rise and Fall of Alexandria—Birthplace of the Modern World*, Justin Pollard and Howard Reid, Penguin Books, 2006, p. 99.

(3) *The Catholic Encyclopedia*, Vol. XII, 1911, article "Pythagoras and Pythagoreanism," pp. 587-588. Also *History of Philosophy*, William S. Sahakian, Barnes and Noble, 1968, pp. 20-23.

(4) *The Five Great Dialogues*, Plato, editor: Louise R, Loomis, Walter J. Black, INC, 1942, Introduction, pp. 3-7.

(5) *History of Philosophy*, William S. Sahakian, Barnes and Noble Books, 1968, pp. 30-33.

(6) *Phaedo, The Five Great Dialogues*, Plato, Walter J. Black, INC, 1942, p. 93.

(7) Ibid., p. 97.

(8) *Timaeus and Critias*, Plato, translator: Desmond Lee, Penguin Books, 1977. A summation of Plato's teachings in Timaeus is found in the Introduction to *The Five Great Dialogues*, pp.12-13, by Louise R, Loomis.

(9) *Republic*, Book X, *The Five Great Dialogues*, Plato, Walter J. Black, INC, 1942, pp. 485-486.

(10) *History of Philosophy*, William S. Sahakian, Barnes and Noble Books, 1968, pp. 57-61.

(11) Ibid., pp. 62-63.

(12) Acts 17:16-34.

(13) *History of Philosophy*, William S. Sahakian, Barnes and Noble Books, 1968, pp. 37-41.

(14) Ibid., pp. 44-47.

(15) *The Hellenistic Age*, Peter Green, Modern Library Edition, 2007, pp. 8-9.

(16) *Antiquities of the Jews*, Flavius Josephus, Book XI, ch. VIII, *Josephus—Complete Works*, translator: William Whiston, Kregel, 1981, pp. 243-244.

(17) *The Hellenistic Age*, Peter Green, Modern Library Edition, 2007, p. 16.

(18) Ibid. Peter Green supplies a detailed history of this era of the Greek Empire.

(19) Ibid., p. 95.

(20) *Imperial Rome*, Moses Hadas, Time Inc., 1965, p. 11.

(21) *Classical Greece*, C. M. Bowra, Time Inc., 1965, p. 11.

(22) *Every Good Man is Free*, v. 13, *The Works of Philo*, translator: C.D. Yonge, Hendrickson Publishers, Inc., 1993, p. 683.

(23) Ibid., v. 2, p. 682.

(24) *On the Creation*, vv. 134-135, The Works of Philo, p. 19.

(25) *Allegorical Interpretation I*, vv. 105-107, The Works of Philo, p. 37

4. The Legacy of Romulus and Remus

(1) *The Lives of the Noble Grecians and Romans*, Plutarch, *Encyclopedia Britannica* edition, 1952, p. 538.

(2) *Imperial Rome*, Moses Hadas, Time Inc., 1965, pp. 44, 57.

(3) Ibid., p. 149.

(4) Ibid., p. 147.

(5) Ibid., p. 83.

(6) Ibid., p. 84.

(7) Ibid., p. 80.

(8) *Rome and Jerusalem: The Clash of Ancient Civilizations*, Martin Goodman, Alfred A. Knopf, 2007, p. 205. Goodman states: "In the late Republic and early empire, divorce was so common among the aristocrats that Roman practice appears less like monogamy than serial polygamy, one spouse at a time, but it would be wrong to assume as general in the wider population behavior that, at times at least, was generated more by political than domestic concerns..."

(9) Ibid., pp. 233-235.

(10) *The Rise of Christianity*, Rodney Stark, Harper Collins, 1997, pp. 97-98.

(11) *Rome and Jerusalem*, p. 206.

(12) *Imperial Rome*, pp. 81-82.

(13) Ibid., pp. 86-88 and *Rome and Jerusalem*, p. 274.

(14) *Rome and Jerusalem*, pp. 281-282.

(15) *Imperial Rome*, p. 121.

(16) Ibid., pp. 123-126.

(17) Ibid., p. 125.

(18) Ibid., p. 127.

(19) *A History of Western Philosophy*, Bertrand Russell, Simon and Schuster, 1972, p. 254.

(20) Ibid., pp. 255-256.

(21) Ibid., pp. 258-259.

5. A Rabbi Named Jesus

(1) *Antiquities of the Jews*, Book XV, ch. IX, v. 6, Josephus, *Josephus—Complete Works*, translator: William Whiston, Kregel, 1981, p. 331. See *National Geographic*, article: "Caesarea Maritima," Robert L. Hohlfelder, February 1987.

(2) Luke 2:41-47.

(3) Matthew 1-2.

(4) Matthew 3.

(5) Matthew 5-7.

(6) *1 Maccabees* 1, *New Jerusalem Bible*, 1990.

(7) *1 Maccabees* 2:42, *New Jerusalem Bible*, 1990, see note 2a.

(8) *The Interpreter's Dictionary of the Bible*, Vol. 3, Abington, 1962, article "Pharisees" by Matthew Black, p. 776.

(9) Deuteronomy 17:8-13.

(10) *Antiquities of the Jews*, Book XVII, ch. II, v. 4, Josephus, p. 358.

(11) *The Life and Times of Jesus the Messiah*, Vol. 1, Book III, ch. II, Alfred Edersheim, Hendrickson, p. 312.

(12) *Wars of the Jews*, Book II, ch. VII, v. 14, Josephus, p. 478.

(13) Acts 23:8.

(14) Matthew 15:1-9. *Jewish New Testament Commentary*, David Stern, Jewish New Testament Publications, Inc., 1992, p. 92.

(15) *The Oxford Companion to the Bible*, Oxford University Press, 1993, article "Corban" by Etienne Trocme, p. 134.

(16) Matthew 12:10-14.

(17) *A Pleasing Fragrance*, Fragment 2, v. 1, *The Dead Sea Scrolls Uncovered*, Barnes and Noble Books, 1992, Robert Eisenman and Michael Wise, p. 204.

(18) *The Life and Times of Jesus the Messiah*, Vols. 1-2, Alfred Edersheim, Hendrickson, Appendix XVII, pp. 777-787. Edersheim summarizes the scores of Talmudic Sabbath regulations.

(19) Matthew 23.

(20) Matthew 5:3-10.

(21) Matthew 7:1-2.

(22) Matthew 7:21-23.

(23) Matthew 10:32-36.

(24) Matthew 18:3.

(25) Matthew 18:8.

(26) Matthew 18:22.

(27) Matthew 19:9.

(28) Matthew 19:16-19.

(29) Matthew 19:23-24.

(30) Matthew 20:27-28.

(31) Matthew 22:36-40.

(32) *The Interpreter's Dictionary of the Bible*, Vol. 4, Abingdon, 1962, article "Sadducees" by A.C. Sundberg, pp. 160-163.

(33) *Antiquities of the Jews*, Book XVII, ch. X, v. 6, Josephus, p. 281.

(34) Matthew 22:23-33; Mark 12:18-27; Luke 20:27-40; Acts 4:1-2. Also, *Wars of the Jews*, Book II, ch. VII, v. 14, Josephus, p. 478. Josephus writes that the Sadducees "take away the belief in the duration of the immortal duration of the soul, and the punishments and rewards of Hades."

(35) Acts 23:8.

(36) *Antiquities of the Jews*, Book II, ch. X, v. 6, Josephus, p. 478.

(37) Matthew 22:23-33; Luke 20:1-39.

(38) *Wars of the Jews*, Book II, ch. VII, v, 1-13, Josephus, pp. 476-478.

(39) *The Messiah of Heaven and Earth*, Fragment 1, vv. 1-2, *The Dead Sea Scrolls Uncovered*, Barnes and Noble Books, 1992, Robert Eisenman and Michael Wise, p. 23. These verses state, "The Heavens and the earth will obey His Messiah and all that is in them. He will not turn aside from the commandments of the Holy Ones." Verse 12 claims that the Messiah will resurrect the dead.

(40) *Abot* 1:12-14, *The Wisdom of Israel*, Lewis Browne, Random House, 1945, pp. 128-129.

(41) *Shabbat* 31b, *The Wisdom of Israel*, p. 131.

6. The Jewish Messiah

(1) Luke 4:16-30.

(2) Matthew 4:17. The phrase "kingdom of heaven" is unique to Matthew. The other gospel writers use "the kingdom of God."

(3) Matthew 16:13-16.

(4) John 11.

(5) John 6.

(6) Isaiah 2:1-4.

(7) *The Jewish Encyclopedia.com*, article "Messiah," by Joseph Jacobs and Moses Buttenweiser.

(8) *The Messiah of Heaven and Earth*, Fragment 1, vv. 1-2, *The Dead Sea Scrolls Uncovered*, Barnes and Noble Books, 1992, Robert Eisenman and Michael Wise, p. 23.

(9) *The Wars of the Jews*, Book VI, ch. V, v. 4, *Josephus—Complete Works*, translator: William Whiston, Kregel, 1981, p. 583. See *Histories*, Book Five, v. 13, Tacitus, Penguin Books, 1993, pp. 287-288.

(10) Luke 2:21-35; Isaiah 42:1-9.

(11) Matthew 24:1-3.

(12) Matthew 24:4-14.

(13) Matthew 24:21-22.

(14) Matthew 24:29-30.

(15) Matthew 25:1-13.

(16) Matthew 25:14-30.

(17) Matthew 25:31-46.

(18) Luke 17:20-21.

(19) The New Revised Standard Version translates this phrase as "the kingdom of God is among you." The New American Standard Bible as "the kingdom of God is in your midst." See *Vine's Expository Dictionary of Biblical Words*, "Within," Vine, Unger and White, Thomas Nelson Publishers, 1985, p. 680.

(20) Exodus 11-12.

(21) Matthew 26:17-30. There is some debate on whether this was a Passover meal, but Matthew, Mark and Luke all call this meal the Passover: Mark 14, Luke 22.

(22) Jeremiah 31:31-33.

(23) *Our Father Abraham, Jewish Roots of the Christian Faith*, Marvin R. Wilson, Eerdmans Publishing Co. 1989, p. 55.

(24) John 1:29; 1 Corinthians 5:7; John 6.

(25) Hebrews 8-10.

(26) Luke 23:6-12.

(27) Acts 1:15.

(28) Acts 2.

(29) Acts 2:41.

(30) Acts 13:42-44; Acts 17:1-4; Acts 18:1-4.

(31) Matthew 28:16-20.

(32) *Popular Mechanics*, December 2002, article "What Did Jesus Look Like?" by Mike Fillon. See author's article "What did Jesus Look Like?" in *The Good News Magazine*, March-April 2004.

(33) Luke 4:28-30; Matthew 26:47-49.

(34) 1 Corinthians 11:14.

(35) Numbers 6:1-6.

7. Growth of the Jesus Sect

(1) Acts 2:1-37.

(2) Acts 2:38.

(3) *The Interpreter's Dictionary of the Bible*, Vol. 4, Abingdon, 1962, article "Repentance," pp. 33-34.

(4) *Vine's Expository Dictionary of Biblical Words*, Vine, Unger and White, Thomas Nelson Publishers, 1985, p. 50 states: "'baptisma,'" consisting of the process of immersion, submersion and emergence."

(5) Acts 8:5-12.

(6) Acts 8:14-17.

(7) Judges 14:19.

(8) *The Interpreter's Dictionary of the Bible*, Vol. 2, Abingdon, 1962, article "Holy Spirit," pp. 626-630.

(9) Psalm 51:11.

(10) Ezekiel 37:1-14; Joel 2:21-3:1.

(11) Jeremiah 31:31-33.

(12) Genesis 17:9-14. Philo defends circumcision for numerous health reasons and then concludes that it is a symbol of 1) "... the excision of the pleasures which delude the mind;" and, 2) "...man's knowing himself..." (*The Special Laws, I, The Works of Philo*, vv. 1-11, translator: C. D. Yonge, Hendrickson Publishers, Inc., 1993, p. 534). Josephus defended two soldiers on whom Jews wanted to compel circumcision with the argument, "Every one ought to worship God according to his own inclinations, and not to be constrained by force..." (*The Life of Flavius Josephus*, Josephus, Kregel Publications, translator: William Whiston, 1981, v. 23).

(13) Deuteronomy 30:6.

(14) Colossians 2:11-12.

(15) Romans 6:1-6.

(16) Acts 2-6.

(17) Acts 6:1-8.

(18) Acts 6-7.

(19) Acts 10:1-11:18.

(20) *The Rise of Christianity*, Rodney Stark, Harper Collins, 1996, p. 57.

(21) *Rome and Jerusalem: The Clash of Ancient Civilizations*, Martin Goodman, Alfred A. Knopf, 2007, p. 271.

(22) *The Special Laws, I, The Works of Philo*, vv. 51-53, translator: C. D. Yonge, Hendrickson Publishers, Inc., 1993, pp. 538-539.

(23) *The Interpreter's Dictionary of the Bible*, Vol. 3, Abingdon, 1962, article "Proselyte," pp. 928-929.

(24) *Antiquities of the Jews*, Josephus, Book XIV, ch. VII, v. 2, *Josephus—Complete Works*, translator: William Whiston, Kregel, 1981, p. 295.

(25) *Histories*, Book Five, vv. 4-5, Tacitus, Penguin Books, 1993, pp. 281-282.

(26) *On the Life of Moses, II, The Works of Philo*, vv. 215-216, 510.

(27) Deuteronomy 5:12-15. See also Deuteronomy 24:14-18.

(28) Exodus 12:43-49; Numbers 15:1-16, esp. vv. 13-16.

(29) Leviticus 24:16-22.

(30) Matthew 1:5.

(31) Isaiah 56:6-8.

(32) Acts 11:26.

(33) *The Rise of Christianity*, Rodney Stark, Harper Collins, 1996, pp. 149-150.

(34) Ibid., pp. 151-156.

(35) Ibid., p. 159.

(36) Acts 8:1-4; 9:1-2.

(37) Acts 9:11; 21:39; 23:33-34.

(38) *The Interpreter's Dictionary of the Bible*, Vol. 4, Abingdon, 1962, article "Tarsus," pp. 518-519.

(39) Acts 21:39-22:3.

(40) Acts 5:34-40.

(41) *Mishna, The Wisdom of Israel*, Lewis Browne, Random House, 1945, p. 179.

(42) *Interpreter's Dictionary of the Bible*, Vol. 2, Abington, 1962, Blair, E.P., article "Gamaliel," p. 351.

(43) Acts 23:6; Acts 26:1-5; Philippians 3:3-6; Acts 8:1-3; Acts 21:39-22:5; Galatians 1:13-14. In Acts 26:9-11 Paul recounts his persecution of the church. The statement "I cast my vote against them" in verse 10 implies possible membership in the Sanhedrin.

(44) Acts 18:1-3; *Mishna, The Wisdom of Israel*, p. 180.

(45) Acts 17:23-34; Titus 1:12.

(46) Acts 16:37; Acts 22:25-28.

(47) 2 Corinthians 10:10.

(48) Acts 9:1-19.

8. Simon, Samaritans and Syncretism

(1)   1 Kings 12:25-33; 1 Kings 14:1-18.

(2)   *Keil & Delitzsch Commentary on the Old Testament*, Vol. 3, C.F Keil and F. Delitzsch, Hendrickson Publications, 1996, p. 187.

(3)   1 Kings 20:23.

(4) 2 Kings 17:26-41.

(5) Ezra 4:1-16.

(6) *Antiquities of the Jews*, Book XI, ch. VIII, v. 6, Josephus, *Josephus—Complete Works*, translator: William Whiston, Kregel, 1981, p. 244.

(7) Luke 9:51-56.

(8) Luke 10:25-37; Luke 17:11-19; Acts 1:8.

(9) John 4:1-26.

(10) Acts 8:9-25.

(11) *The History of the Church*, Eusebius, translator: G.A. Williamson, Dorset Press, 1965, pp. 73-74, 85-87, 135-136. There is controversy surrounding Justin's (*Apology I*, ch. 25) claim that a statue in the Tiber River was dedicated to Simon the Magician of Acts 8. A statue bearing the inscription has been discovered, though many historians believe that the statue in question was dedicated to a local god, not Simon.

(12) *Encyclopedia Britannica*, Vol. XXII, New Werner Edition, 1907, p. 87. (See *Against Heresies*, Ireneus, Book 1, ch. 23, The Ante-Nicene Fathers, Vol. I, translator: Alexander Roberts, editors: Alexander Roberts and James Donaldson, American Edition, 1979.)

(13) Ibid.

(14) *The Apocryphon of John*, *The Nag Hammadi Library*, editor: James M. Robinson, Harper & Row, 1988, pp. 104-123.

(15) *The History of the Church*, Eusebius, translator: G.A. Williamson, Dorset Press, 1965, pp. 86-87.

(16) Ibid., pp. 73-74.

(17) Acts 17:21.

(18) *Catholic Encyclopedia*, Vol. 13, Robert Appleton Company, 1912, article "Simon Magus," pp. 797-798.

(19) *The Acts of Peter, Lost Scriptures*, editor: Bart D. Ehrman, Oxford University Press, 2003, pp. 135-154.

(20) This article appeared in an earlier version in *Ministerial Journal* published by the United Church of God, *aia*.

9. Turning the World Upside Down

(1) Acts 9:1-32.

(2) Acts 13:1-5.

(3) Acts 13:14-41, esp. vv. 38-39.

(4) Acts 13:42-52.

(5) Acts 14:1-6.

(6) *The Rise of Christianity*, W.H.C. Frend, Fortress Press, 1984, pp. 99-100.

(7) Galatians 4:22-31.

(8) Romans 3:4, 10-18; 9:25-26, 27-29, 33; 10:19-21; 11:2-4, 8-9, 26-27, 34-35; 14:11; 15:9-12, 21.

(9) Acts 15:1-6.

(10) Acts 15:7-11.

(11) Acts 15:15-21.

(12) *Jewish New Testament Commentary*, David Stern, Jewish New Testament Publications, Inc., 1992, pp. 277-279. Stern lists the common interpretations of this passage.

(13) Ibid.

(14) Galatians 5:19-21.

(15) 1 Corinthians 6:9-11.

(16) Acts 15:30-41.

(17) Acts 16:13-15.

(18) Acts 17:1-6.

(19) Acts 17:11-12.

(20) Acts 17:15-27.

(21) *The Lives of the Noble Grecians and Romans*, Plutarch, Encyclopedia Britannica, Inc., 1952, p. 68.

(22) Acts 17:28-34.

(23) *Jewish New Testament Commentary*, David Stern, Jewish New Testament Publication, Inc., 1992, pp. 297-298. Although Stern comes to the conclusion that the New Testament doesn't command a specific day of worship for Christians, he gives a credible explanation of why this passage is referring to a Saturday night.

(24) Acts 20:7-12.

(25) David Stern, in *Jewish New Testament Commentary*, makes this observation: "*Motza'ei-Shabbat* in Hebrew means "departure of the Sabbath" and refers to Saturday night. The Greek text here says, "the first day of the *sabbaton*," where Greek *sabbaton* transliterates Hebrew *Shabbat* and may be translated "Sabbath" or "week," depending upon the context. Since *Shabbat* itself is only one day, "the first day of the *sabbaton*" must be the first day of the week" (pp. 297-298).

10. The Wisdom of the World

(1) *The Oxford Companion to the Bible*. Oxford University Press, 1993, article "Corinth" by Richard E. Oster, Jr., pp. 134-135.

(2) Acts 18:1-11.

(3) 1 Corinthians 1:18-22, esp. v. 22.

(4) 1 Corinthians 1:23-31.

(5) 1 Corinthians 3:18-19.

(6) 1 Corinthians 2:6-16.

(7) 1 Corinthians 10:21-23.

(8) 1 Corinthians 1:19, 31; 2:9; 3:19-20; 6:16; 9:9; 10:1-11; 14:21; 15:3.

(9) 1 Corinthians 5:6-8.

(10) 1 Corinthians 7:19.

(11) 1 Corinthians 15:1-20.

(12) 1 Corinthians 15:21-44, esp. vv. 41-44.

(13) 1 Corinthians 15:41-58, esp. vv. 51-53.

(14) 1 Corinthians 9:19-21.

(15) 2 Corinthians 3:1-3.

(16) Ezekiel 11:19-21; 36:22-27.

(17) 2 Corinthians 3:4-6. Paul develops this theme further in Romans 2:25-29; 7:7-25; and 8:1-11.

(18) Exodus 34:29-35.

(19) 2 Corinthians 3:7-18. For a similar explanation of this passage see *The International Critical Commentary: The Epistle to the Romans*, Vol. II, C.E.B Cranfield, T&T Clark, Edinburgh, 1994, pp. 853-857.

11. A Deranged Emperor and the Destruction of the Jewish Temple

(1) Acts 18:2.

(2) *The Lives of the Twelve Caesars*, Suetonius, The Heritage Press, 1965, pp. 309-360. Also *The Annals of Imperial Rome*, Tacitus, Dorset Press, 1984, pp. 252-397.

(3) *The Annals of Imperial Rome*, Tacitus, Dorset Press, 1984, pp. 362-363.

(4) Ibid., p. 365.

(5) Ibid., pp. 365-366.

(6) *The Lives of the Twelve Caesars*, p. 321.

(7) *Dio's Roman History*, Dio, VIII, Books LXI-LXX, translator: E. Cary, Leob Classical Library, 1968, p. 115.

(8) 2 Chronicles 28:1-3; 33:1-6; 2 Kings 23:10.

(9) Jeremiah 7:30-34.

(10) *Nelson's New Illustrated Bible Dictionary*, editor: Ronald F. Youngblood, Thomas Nelson Publishers, 1995, article "Hinnom, Valley of," p. 568.

(11) Matthew 5:29-30.

(12) Matthew 10:28.

(13) 2 Peter 3:10.

(14) Revelation 20:13-15.

(15) Revelation 21:1-7.

(16) *The Wars of the Jews*, Book VI, ch. III, v. 3, *Josephus—Complete Works*, translator: William Whiston, Kregel, 1981, p. 578.

(17) *The Wars of the Jews*, Book VI, ch. IX, v. 3, p. 587. Tacitus puts the total number of people in Jerusalem during the siege as 600,000. See *The Histories*, Book V, v. 13, Tacitus, Penguin Books, 1993, p. 288.

(18) Acts 24:5.

(19) *The History of the Church*, Eusebius, Dorset Press, 1984, p. 111.

(20) *Encyclopedia Britannica*, Vol. XVII, New Werner Edition, 1907, article "Nazarenes," pp. 311-312.

(21) *The Wars of the Jews*, Book VI, ch. V, v. 3, p. 582.

(22) *Histories*, Book Five, v. 13, Tacitus, Penguin Books, 1993, pp. 287-288.

(23) Hebrews 1:1-2.

(24) Hebrews 1-2.

(25) Hebrews 7 (notice v. 12).

(26) Hebrews 7:26-27; Hebrews 9.

(27) Hebrews 8.

(28) Hebrews 6:1-2.

12. Why Become a Christian?

(1) *A History of Private Life, Vol. 1: From Pagan Rome to Byzantium*, translator: Arthur Goldhammer, editor: Paul Veyne, Balkan Harvard Press, 1987, p. 219.

(2) *The Rise of Christianity*, Rodney Stark, Harper Collins, 1996, pp. 86-88.

(3) Galatians 3:26-29.

(4) Philemon vv. 1-25.

(5) *A History of Private Life, Vol. 1: From Pagan Rome to Byzantium*, p. 51.

(6) Ibid., pp. 52-61. The author later notes on page 68 that "The right of legal marriage was given to slaves around 200 AD".

(7) *Historical Selections*, editor: Hutton Webster, D.C. Heath and Company, 1929, "Seneca on the Treatment of Slaves," pp. 204-205.

(8) Ibid.

(9) Ephesians 6:5-9; Colossians 3:22-4:1.

(10) Philemon vv. 1-25.

(11) *A History of Private Life, Vol. 1: From Pagan Rome to Byzantium*, pp. 219-223.

(12) *The Wars of the Jews*, Book VI, ch. I, v. 5, *Josephus—Complete Works*, translator: William Whiston, Kregel, 1981, p. 572.

(13) Romans 2:5-7.

(14) 1 Corinthians 15.

(15) 2 Corinthians 4:3-4.

(16) Ephesians 2:1-3.

(17) Ephesians 6:12.

(18) *The Decline and Fall of the Roman Empire*, Vol. 1, Edward Gibbon, The Modern Library, p. 383.

(19) Acts 20:29-30.

(20) 2 Peter 2:1-2.

(21) 1 John 4:1.

(22) Revelation 2-3.

13. Persecution, Forgeries and Gnostics

(1) *1 Clement* 53:1-2, *Lost Scriptures*, editor: Bart D. Ehrman, Oxford University Press, 2003, pp. 180-181.

(2) *The Didache, Lost Scriptures*, editor: Bart D. Ehrman, Oxford University Press, 2003, pp. 211-217.

(3) Ibid., ch. 8, vv. 1-3, pp. 214-215.

(4) *Epistle to the Trallians, Early Christian Writings: The Apostolic Fathers*, Ignatius, Dorset Press, 1986, p. 97.

(5) *Epistle to Rome, Early Christian Writings: The Apostolic Fathers*, Ignatius, Dorset Press, 1986, pp. 102-108.

(6) *Readings In Ancient History: Rome*, editor: William Stearns Davis, Allyn and Bacon, 1913, pp. 219-222.

(7) *Dio's Roman History*, Dio, VIII, Books LXI-LXX, translator: E. Cary, Leob Classical Library, 1968, pp. 421-423.

(8) Ibid.

(9) *The History of the Church*, Eusebius, Dorset Press, 1984, pp. 154-155.

(10) *Dio's Roman History*, VIII, p. 447.

(11) Ibid., pp. 447-451. Dio puts Jewish battle deaths alone at 580,000.

(12) 2 Peter 3:16.

(13) 2 Thessalonians 2:2.

(14) Acts 4:36-37; 11:19-30; 13:1-3.

(15) *The Epistle of Barnabas*, 15:1-9; *Lost Scriptures*, editor: Bart D. Ehrman, Oxford University Press, 2003, p. 232.

(16) Ibid., 4:7-8, p. 222.

(17) Ibid., 10:1-12, pp. 227-228.

(18) *The History of the Church*, Eusebius, Dorset Press, 1984, pp. 138-139, 167.

(19) *History of Philosophy*, William S. Sahakian, Barnes and Noble Books, 1968, pp. 52-61.

(20) *Against Heresies*, Ireneus, "Carpocrates," Book 1, ch. XXV, vv. 1-4, pp. 350-351. *The Ante-Nicene Fathers*, Vol. 1, editors: Alexander Roberts and James Donaldson, American Edition, 1979.

(21) *Against Heresies*, Ireneus, "Cainites," Book 1, ch. XXXI, v. 1, p. 358. *The Ante-Nicene Fathers*, Vol. 1, editors: Alexander Roberts and James Donaldson, American Edition, 1979.

(22) *The Exegesis of the Soul*, *The Nag Hammadi Library*, Harper and Row, 1988, pp. 192-198.

(23) *The History of the Church*, Eusebius, pp. 136-137. Ehrman has a translation of the fragments of *The Gospel of the Ebionites in Lost Scriptures*. Although Ehrman's conclusions concerning early Christianity are highly debatable, he supplies a good explanation of the polar views of the Ebionites and Marcionites in *Lost Christianities* (Oxford University Press, 2003).

(24) *The Early Church*, *The Pelican History of the Church* Vol. 1, Henry Chadwick, Pelican Books, 1985, pp. 39-40.

(25) *Against Heresies*, Ireneus, "Doctrines of Cerdo and Marcion," Book 1, ch. XXVII, vv. 1-4, pp. 352-353.

(26) *A History of the Church*, Paul Johnson, Touchstone, 1976, p. 46.

(27) *The Infancy Gospel of Thomas*, chs. 1-9, *Lost Scriptures*, editor: Bart D. Ehrman, Oxford University Press, 2003, pp. 58-60.

(28) *The Jewish Encyclopedia.com*, 2002, article "Bar Kokba and Bar Kokba War," Richard Gottheil and Samuel Krauss.

(29) *The History of the Church*, Eusebius, pp. 156-157.

14. The Eighth Day and Quartodecimens

(1) Luke 4:16, 42-44; John 18:20; Acts 2:1-2; 9:2; 13:1-5, 13-44; 14:1; 16:11-13; 17:1-4, 16-17; 18:1-7, 24-26; Romans 16:5; Colossians 4:15. For instructions to church leaders see Paul's writings in 1 Timothy 3 and Titus 1.

(2) *Readings In Ancient History: Rome*, editor: William Stearns Davis, Allyn and Bacon, 1913, pp. 219-222.

(3) *The First Apology of Justin*, Justin Martyr, ch. 67, *The Ante-Nicene Fathers*, Vol. I, translator: Alexander Roberts, editors: Alexander Roberts and James Donaldson, American Edition, 1979, pp. 185-186.

(4) *The Rise of Christianity*, W.H.C. Frend, Fortress Press, 1984, p. 297.

(5) *The History of the Church*, Eusebius, Dorset Press, 1984, p. 404.

(6) *Dialogue with Trypho*, Justin Martyr, *The Ante-Nicene Fathers*, Vol. I, translator: Alexander Roberts, editors: Alexander Roberts and James Donaldson, American Edition, 1979, pp. 204-205.

(7) Ibid., p., 200.

(8) Ibid., p. 218.

(9) *The Epistle of Barnabas*, 15:1-9, *Lost Scriptures*, editor: Bart D. Ehrman, Oxford University Press, 2003, pp. 232-233.

(10) *Dialogue with Trypho*, Justin Martyr, ch. XXIV, *Ante-Nicene Fathers*, Vol. I, American Edition, editors: Alexander Roberts and James Donaldson, American Edition, 1979, p. 206.

(11) Ibid., ch. XLI, p. 215 and ch. CXXXVIII, p. 268.

(12) *The Stromata, or Miscellanies*, Clement of Alexander, Book 5, ch. 14, *Ante-Nicene Fathers*, Vol. II, American Edition, editors: Alexander Roberts and James Donaldson, 1979, p. 469.

(13) *The History of the Church*, Eusebius, Dorset Press, 1984, p. 233.

(14) *The Epistle of Polycarp to the Philippians*, *Early Christian Writings: The Apostolic Fathers*, Dorset Press, 1986, pp. 144-150.

(15) *The Martyrdom of Polycarp*, *Early Christian Writings: The Apostolic Fathers*, Dorset Press, 1986, pp. 155-164.

(16) *The Encyclopedia Britannica* states, "There is no trace of the celebration of Easter as a Christian festival in the New Testament or in the writings of the apostolic fathers....The first Christians, being derived from, or intimately connected with, the Jewish Church, naturally continued to observe the Jewish festivals, though in a new spirit, as commemoration of events

that these had been the shadows. The Passover, ennobled by the thought of Christ the true Paschal Lamb, the first fruits of the dead, continued to be celebrated, and became the Christian Easter." (*New Werner Edition Encyclopedia Britannica*, Vol. VII, The Werner Company, 1907, article "Easter," p. 531.)

(17) *The Early Church, The Pelican History of the Church*, Vol. 1, Henry Chadwick, Pelican Books, 1985, pp. 84-85.

(18) *The History of the Church*, Eusebius, Dorset Press, 1984, pp. 230-232.

(19) *The Rise of Christianity*, W.H.C. Frend, Fortress Press, 1984, pp. 256-257.

(20) *The First Apology of Justin*, Justin Martyr, chs. 5-6, *The Ante-Nicene Fathers*, Vol. I, translator: Alexander Roberts, editors: Alexander Roberts and James Donaldson, American Edition, 1979, p. 164. Justin Martyr responded to the accusation that the rejection of Greek and Roman gods was atheism: "Hence are we called atheists. And we confess that we are atheists, so far as gods of this sort are concerned, but not with respect to the most true God, the Father of righteousness and temperance and the other virtues, who is free from all impurity. But both Him, and the Son (who came forth from Him and taught us these things, and the host of the other good angels who follow and are made like to Him), and the prophetic Spirit, we worship and adore, knowing them in reason and truth, and declaring without grudging to everyone who wishes to learn, as we have been taught."

(21) *The Lives of the Twelve Caesars*, Suetonius, The Heritage Press, 1965, p. 321.

15. Hellenized Orthodoxy

(1) *The Rise and Fall of Alexandria: Birthplace of the Modern World*, Justin Pollard and Howard Reid, Penguin Books, 2006, pp. 2-3.

(2) Ibid., pp. xiii-xiv.

(3) *The Rise of Christianity*, W.H.C. Frend, Fortress Press, 1984, p. 35.

(4) Ibid., pp. 205-210.

(5) *History of Philosophy*, William S. Sahakian, Barnes and Noble, 1968, pp. 80-85.

(6) *The Stromata, or Miscellanies*, Clement of Alexandria, Book I, ch. 5, *Ante-Nicene Fathers*, Vol. 2, American Edition, editors: Alexander Roberts and James Donaldson, 1979, p. 305.

(7) Ibid., ch. VII, p. 308.

(8) Ibid., ch. XXV, p. 338. This was not a new idea; Justin Martyr wrote that Plato had borrowed his ideas from Moses. See *The First Apology of Justin*, Justin Martyr, *Ante-Nicene Fathers*, Vol. 1, American Edition, editors: Alexander Roberts and James Donaldson, 1979, pp. 182-183.

(9) *On First Principles*, Origen, Book 1, ch. 7, vv. 2-5, *Ante-Nicene Fathers*, Vol. 4, American Edition, editors: Alexander Roberts and James Donaldson, 1979, p. 263. Origen states: "We think, then, that they [sun, moon and stars] may be designated as living beings, for this reason, that they are said to receive commandments from God, which is ordinarily the case only with rational beings. 'I have given a commandment to all the stars,' says the Lord. What, now, are these commandments? Those, namely, that each star, in its own order and course, should bestow upon the world the amount of splendour which has been entrusted to it." He also states that the Old Testament prophet Jeremiah called the moon the "Queen of Heaven." This reference is probably to Jeremiah 7:18.

(10) Ibid., Book I, ch. VI, pp. 260-262.

(11) Ibid., Book IV, ch. I, v. 22, p. 371.

(12) Ibid., Book I, chs. I-III, pp. 242-256.

(13) *A History of Western Philosophy*, Bertrand Russell, Simon and Schuster, 1972, p. 327. See Matthew 19:11-12.

(14) *Against Praxeas*, Tertullian, chs. 2-3, *Ante-Nicene Fathers*, Vol. 3, American Edition, editors: Alexander Roberts and James Donaldson, 1979, pp. 598-599.

(15) *The Apology*, Tertullian, Book IX, "A Treatise on the Soul," chs. LI-LV, *Ante-Nicene Fathers*, Vol. 3, American Edition, editors: Alexander Roberts and James Donaldson, 1979, pp. 228-231.

(16) *The Apology*, Tertullian, Book II, "On Idolatry," ch. XIV, *Ante-

Nicene Fathers, Vol. 3, American Edition, editors: Alexander Roberts and James Donaldson, 1979, pp. 69-70.

(17) *Eerdmans' Handbook to the History of Christianity*, Lion Publishing, 1977, article "The Montanists," by David F. Wright, p. 74.

(18) *Imperial Rome*, Moses Hadas, Time Inc., 1965, pp. 141-142.

(19) *The Rise of Christianity*, W.H.C. Frend, Fortress Press, 1984, pp. 308, 440.

(20) Ibid., pp. 341-343.

(21) Ibid., p. 368.

(22) *The Catholic Encyclopedia*, Vol. IX, Robert Appleton Company, 1910, article "Manichaeism," by J.P. Arendzen, p. 591.

(23) Ibid., pp. 592-593.

(24) *The Catholic Encyclopedia*, Vol. X, Robert Appleton Company, 1911, article "Mithraism," by J. P. Arendzen, pp. 402-404.

16. Hellenized Christianity Triumphant

(1) *Constantine the Great: The Man and His Times*, Michael Grant, Charles Scribner's Sons, 1993, p. 38.

(2) Ibid., pp. 138-141

(3) Ibid., p. 143.

(4) *Encyclopedia Britannica, New Werner Edition*, Vol. VI, 1907, article "Constantine I," p. 268.

(5) *The History of the Church*, Eusebius, Dorset Press, 1984, pp. 401-404.

(6) Ibid., pp. 405-406.

(7) Ibid., pp. 407-408.

(8) *Documents of the Christian Church*, editor: Henry Bettenson, Oxford University Press, 1967, pp. 18-19.

(9) Ibid., p. 19.

(10) An interesting exploration of the effects of Gnosticism and Hellenism on Primitive Christianity can be found in *Primitive Christianity in Crisis* by Alan Knight, A.R.K. Research, 2003.

(11) *A History of Christianity*, Paul Johnson, Touchstone, 1976, pp. 37-38.

(12) Galatians 3:22.

(13) Galatians 2:15-16.

(14) Galatians 2:17-21.

(15) Galatians 3-4.

(16) 1 Corinthians 7:19.

(17) *Against Heresies*, Irenaeus, Book IV, ch. XV, v. 1, *The Ante-Nicene Fathers*, Vol. 1, editors: Alexander Roberts and James Donaldson, American Edition, 1979, p. 479.

(18) Ibid., ch. XVI, v. 4, p. 482.

(19) Ibid., ch. XVI, vv. 1-2, pp. 480-481.

(20) *The Early Church, The Pelican History of the Church*, Vol. 1, Henry Chadwick, Pelican Books, 1985, p. 126.

(21) Ibid., pp. 126-127.

Printed in Great Britain
by Amazon

48864671R00120